NICHOLLS, David. The pluralist state. St. Martin's, 1975. 179p bibl 74-23710. 18.95

Nicholls (chaplain and fellow of Exeter College, Oxford) in this book continues his work in the area of pluralism begun earlier in *Three varieties of pluralism* (CHOICE, Jul.-Aug. 1975) and in numerous articles. The work is concerned with a group of English political thinkers known as pluralists (Figgis, Maitland, Acton, Laski, Cole, Russell, etc.). The book presents the ideas of these men, concentrating on Figgis. Topics treated include: liberty, the attack on sovereignty, group personality, the state, the group, and the individual. It ends with a useful contrast of this pluralist school with other varieties of pluralist thought, particularly American theories of pluralism. The book is a timely treatment of an issue that has received important new analysis recently, i.e., the nature of political obligation. The ideas of the pluralist as analyzed here deserve comparison with those found in John Rawls' *A theory of justice* (CHOICE, Sept. 1972) and Robert Paul Wolff's *In defense of anarchism* (CHOICE, Mar. 1971). The book is readable, scholarly, and reliable. Index; bibliography. Recommended for graduate and undergraduate (upper-division) college libraries.

THE PLURALIST STATE

THE PLURALIST STATE

DAVID NICHOLLS

Chaplain and Fellow
Exeter College, Oxford

ST. MARTIN'S PRESS NEW YORK

AFFILIATED PUBLISHERS: Macmillan Limited, London
also at Bombay, Calcutta, Madras and Melbourne

FOR GILLIE, WITH LOVE

God himself would admit a figure of society, as there is a plurality of persons in God, though there be but one God; and all his external actions testify a love of society and communion. In heaven there are orders of angels, and armies of martyrs, and in that house many mansions; in earth, families, cities, churches, colleges, all plural things; and lest either of these should not be company enough alone, there is an association of both, a communion of saints which makes the militant and triumphant church one parish.

John Donne (1624)

Contents

Preface

I wish to thank the Community of the Resurrection, Mirfield,
Yorkshire, for allowing me to use their library, and for their
hospitality on a number of occasions. This monograph has
benefited greatly from criticisms and suggestions at various
stages of its development. Ernest Thorp, David Price and
Martyn Thompson have made very useful criticisms and I
should particularly mention the help given to me by Alec
Vidler.

For permission to reproduce as appendixes the articles by
J. N. Figgis and H. J. Laski I am grateful respectively to the
Community of the Resurrection and to the editor of the
Philosophical Review.

DAVID NICHOLLS

1 Introduction: Parentalism and Pluralism

If the negative liberalism of Jeremy Bentham, John Bright and Herbert Spencer was the ideology of a developing capitalism, the positive liberalism of T. H. Green, Henry Jones, L. T. Hobhouse and the Webbs was the ideology of established capitalism.[1] It is no accident that Joseph Chamberlain, a leading spokesman from Birmingham, should be one of the first politicians to recognise the need for a new theory of positive state action. In the first part of the nineteenth century the machinery of state — which was still largely controlled by landed interests — was likely to be used to restrict the development of capitalism; the interests of the industrialists were best served by *laissez faire.* By the close of the century the most significant challenges to capitalism were coming, not from the old entrenched agricultural sector, but from trade unions and other groups which refused to accept the new social order. Herbert Spencer, who was so eager to welcome almost every kind of voluntary association, was very suspicious of trade unions; perhaps he could dimly see that they provided a potential challenge to the new society. The state was now largely controlled by members of the bourgeois class, who clearly recognised the positive role which the state itself could play in preserving the society which they had done so much to build. Not only was a strong state needed in order to prevent violent uprisings from working-class groups — the negative liberalism of an earlier generation had insisted that the state should retain this function — but it was increasingly acknowledged that capitalism could survive only if positive action were taken to mitigate some of the harsher features of the new industrial system. This positive action could more efficiently be undertaken by the state than by private agencies. In one western European country after another the state began to take upon itself the role of an anxious parent. Legislation was passed, restricting the hours of work, prohibiting the employment of children, enforcing safety regulations, providing unemployment pay and old age benefits. This 'new Toryism', as Spencer called it, was justified by modifications in the theory of liberalism. To be free to do something, it was suggested, a man must have the power or the means to do it; freedom to act is not ensured simply by the absence of external impediments. Therefore in providing the means of a better life, the state is increasing the *liberty* of the mass of the people.[2] So successful were the positive liberals in transforming liberalism from a doctrine of *laissez faire* to a doctrine of positive state action, that some present-day writers regard the advocacy of this kind of positive state action as the very essence of liberalism. T. Lowi writes of interest group liberalism in the following terms:

> It may be called liberalism because it expects to use government in a positive and expansive role, it is motivated by the highest sentiments, and it possesses strong faith that what is good for government is good for the society.[3]

The positive liberals certainly did a thorough job. The new positive role adopted by the state threw the socialist camp into almost total confusion. Only the bourgeois socialist prophet, from the snug security of his study, could possibly argue that the labour movement should oppose or reject the benefits which were being offered by the state. No one involved in the daily struggle of the movement could realistically think in these terms. Yet it required a William Morris in England and a Rosa Luxemburg in Germany to warn socialists against believing that social reform can properly take the place of social revolution, and that the capitalist state can gradually evolve into a friendly society. The warnings were not heeded. In Germany revisionism carried the day, though Bernstein remained enough of a marxist to criticise the 'eternal heaping of duties on the state'.[4] English Fabians, largely unencumbered by marxist preconceptions, found no problem in welcoming the new Toryism. It was the aim of social democrats, in the words of Bernard Shaw,

Through Democracy to gather the whole people into the
State, so that the State may be trusted with the rent of the
country, and finally with the land, the capital, and the
organization of the national industry — with all the sources
of production, in short, which are now abandoned to the
cupidity of irresponsible private individuals.[5]

Sidney Webb wrote complacently of 'our irresistible glide
into collectivist Socialism',[6] and was unashamedly elitist in
his attitudes. Beatrice used to say that she and her husband
were 'benevolent, bourgeois and bureaucratic', in contrast to
the guild socialists who were 'aristocratic, anarchist and arro-
gant'.[7] Robert Michels observed how most English socialists
thought of democracy in terms of a benevolent despotism.[8]
With the defeat of William Morris and his supporters, at the
famous debate of the Fabians in 1886, English socialists
moved towards bureaucratic parentalism, taking over much
of the ideology of the positive liberals. Nothing was to stand
in the way of the state. The new leviathan, however, was to
be democratically controlled; the will of the people is the will
of God. 'Lewis was shocked,' wrote H. G. Wells of a liberal
politician, in *The New Machiavelli*, 'A "Mandate" from the
country was sacred to his system of pretences.' It is hardly
surprising that Shaw welcomed the advent of Mussolini in
Italy, and that the Webbs became admirers of Stalinism.

The action of the state in exercising compulsion against
people for their own good came to be justified in terms of
helping them to live the life that they would really like to
live, if only they were provident enough; it is one of the
rights of the citizen 'to be protected against his own weaknesses'.[9] Those who did not justify the positive actions of the
state as directly contributing to an increase in human freedom, defended these actions as promoting the general
happiness or realising the common good, a happiness and a
good which were thought in some way or other to be willed
or desired by 'the people'. The paternal state imposes sanctions upon people in order to compel them to act in accordance with their own interests, or to refrain from acting
against these interests. The maternal state goes further; by
anticipating the needs and desires of citizens, it makes provi-

sion for them in such a way that they do not even want to act in a manner which is incompatible with the 'general interest', with which their own interests are said to be inextricably bound up. Paternalism employs the harsh external method of physical sanctions, maternalism adopts a more gentle means of moulding character and of taking away those nasty, awkward, 'anti-social' traits which lead men to question, to challenge and, like the prophets of Israel, to disrupt the comfortable complacency of their neighbours (not by interfering in some direct manner, but merely by being what they are, and by speaking the truth as they see it).

The late nineteenth century was characterised by a growth in nationalism and by governmental insistence that all loyalties must be subordinated to the claims of the national state. Germany and Italy had been united on the basis of nationality, and conscious efforts were being made, particularly in the former, to enlist the support of all subordinate groups and to weld them into a coherent whole. Those groups which insisted on maintaining independence from the government were regarded as subversive, hence Bismarck's attacks on the Roman Catholic Church during the so-called *Kulturkampf*. The dynamic nationalism of a youthful Germany led to demands in other European countries for a more unified state. The virulent anti-clericalism of Emile Combes in France sprang from the same root. Economic policies were adopted in order to strengthen national unity — protection became the order of the day. In the field of education there was the demand that developments were required in order to serve the needs of the state. In England a new emphasis was placed upon technical subjects and upon the natural sciences; these were thought to be more useful than the humanities, and would strengthen the power of the state; the example of Germany was pointed to. The nation state was seen to be the only really important group to which the individual belongs.

It was against this background that pluralism developed. How can we expect this maternalistic state to realise a common good when it is composed of social and economic groups whose interests are often totally incompatible? How can we expect the state to act in the real interests of the masses when its political and administrative machinery is effectively controlled by a small group of persons whose interest it is to preserve the *status quo*, and above all to perpetuate and extend the power of the state itself? How can there be a general happiness which is anything other than the happiness of individuals, and of groups of individuals, pursuing some end which they choose to pursue? How can the state do anything to increase this happiness, other than by allowing people to live their lives as they choose as members of those associations which they desire to join?

By the beginning of the twentieth century it had become clear to a number of thinkers that the only hope for freedom in the modern world was by attacking the outrageous claims being made on behalf of the state. The only factor uniting these thinkers was a refusal to pay homage to the established capitalist system of their day, and a recognition that the parentalist state was rapidly becoming the chief instrument for preserving this system. J. N. Figgis saw clearly that the ascendance of the absolute state in his own day was directly linked to 'the horror of that very economic and industrial oppression which is the distinctive gift of modern capitalism to history'.[10] Many of these thinkers were members of groups whose existence was being challenged by the claims of the state. In France the government was committed to establishing a bourgeois secular society where the corporate claims of the christian churches and of the radical trade unions were alike totally rejected. 'There are and there can be no rights,' wrote M. Emile Combes, 'except the right of the State and there are and can be no other authority than the authority of the Republic'.[11]

In England the situation had developed differently. The Church of England was still seen as a national institution, and in exchange for the privileges involved in this status its spiritual independence in a number of spheres was limited. Trade unions were treated with toleration and even with respect, so long as they concentrated on improving conditions for their members, and accepted the ideology of the welfare state. Nevertheless any action which was thought seriously to threaten the social and economic arrangements of the state was suppressed, while the very desire to make radical changes was eroded by the maternalistic actions of the state.

Elitist thinkers in Italy, France and Germany reminded their contemporaries at the turn of the century that large-scale organisation inevitably involves control by a small elite. But Mosca, Pareto and Michels did little more than repeat in sociological jargon the perceptions of J. F. Stephen, Henry Maine and Arthur Balfour. Democracy would not mean, as J. S.Mill had imagined, the government of each by all the rest, but the government of each by a relatively small group of 'wirepullers'. The result of cutting up voting power into little bits 'is simply that the man who can sweep the greatest number of them into one heap will govern the rest'.[12] Many of these elitist writers believed that the 'iron law of oligarchy' was not only a fact but was a welcome fact. Stephen insisted that bureaucracy was the only hope for a country which paid lip-service to the notion of democracy. He attacked those who feared an increasing centralisation, and argued that we must choose the best servants that we can find and give them the power necessary to do their work. Not only was oligarchy inevitable in the state, but also in any large organisation. Maine and Michels applied the theory specifically to political parties.

Anarchists, of course, shared this perception with elitists; large-scale organisation necessarily involves oligarchy, particularly in the case of compulsory associations like the state. Instead of welcoming oligarchy, which is the invariable companion of organisation, they rejected both. Anarchists insisted that freedom can be preserved only in small voluntary groups, and that mass participation in the politics of a large state is an impossibility. The pluralists — Figgis, Laski, Cole, Russell — accepted the main contention of the anarchists; they believed that men should in general be left to pursue ends chosen by themselves, in the context of voluntary associations. Yet they argued that the state should remain as the society of societies, responsible for maintaining order among the groups within it. The state should not itself, however, pursue a goal or purpose other than that of maintaining a situation where people are able, as individuals and associated in groups, to follow paths which they choose for themselves. How right was Rousseau in his condemnation of representation. True participation can never be achieved though representative government. In the modern state, as Figgis insisted, the mass of people will have nothing to do with the law except to obey it, unless there exist strong local groups having real autonomy. 'The mere fact of a system of so-called representatives will not secure freedom.'[13] Participatory democracy is possible only in small groups.

If Maine and Michels were right in claiming that the iron law of oligarchy applies as much to large organisations within the state as to the state itself, did the pluralists not see that large groups like trade unions and churches constitute a threat to individual freedom in the same way that the state does? Many of them did recognise that any large centralised organisation would invariably be controlled by a small, often self-perpetuating and self-interested, oligarchy; these writers therefore extended their federal ideas to the groups which composed the state. Figgis, for example, was very much concerned with the problem of authority in the church, and warned against the centralising tendencies of Rome. He saw in ultramontanism 'a theory analogous to that which we have been combating in the State'.[14] He argued in favour of power being dispersed within the church among semi-autonomous national churches, and to smaller units like dioceses and monastic communities, and was particularly insistent on stressing the role of *small* groups in the state. His interest in the conciliar theorists of the fifteenth century was not simply in their claim that general councils had greater authority than the pope; these conciliar theories allow for the development of semi-autonomous units within the Catholic Church.[15] G. D. H. Cole and the guild socialists were suspicious of the large trade unions and argued for a system of industrial unionism, where much of the real power would be exercised locally. What most of the pluralists rejected was the idea that the state should interfere with groups in order to protect the interests of members, and impose upon the group the kind of polity which it thought best. So long as people were free to leave, the state should not as a general rule interfere. The really effective claim for freedom and for a devolution of power within the large associations must come from within and not from outside. Only if it comes from the members themselves will it be likely to lead to a real change for the

better; if it comes from the state nothing but state absolutism
can result.

The English pluralists envisaged a situation in which members of the state pursue their chosen ends in life, as individuals and associated in voluntary groups, with as little interference from coercive governmental authorities as is possible
in the context of order and peace. Figgis used the term 'state'
to apply to this collectivity; it is the society of societies,
whose purpose is to maintain some kind of order, and to
adjudicate between the claims made by its members. Individual citizens will naturally join groups, for man is a social
animal. These groups will develop a life of their own, which
cannot be accounted for simply in terms of the actions and
ideas of their individual members. The degree of unity attained by the group will depend upon the nature of the
purpose pursued, and upon the loyalty manifested by its
members. Pluralist writers believed that a permanent association, pursuing a definite purpose upon which its members are
in general agreement, manifests a unity which enables us to
treat it in certain respects as a 'person'. Obviously there are
important ways in which a group differs from an individual
person, but there are certain common features which groups
share with individuals. These groups have an existence which
is not derived from the state. Certainly, they agreed, there
must be some machinery for recognising and registering these
groups, and for settling disputes between them. The law, if it
is to be an effective instrument of social control, must
recognise groups as real entities — as legal persons — but the
life of the groups is not derived from their having been
recognised. Quite the reverse; the law recognises them because they exist as social facts, just as the law recognises
individuals as legal persons. Individual citizens will normally
belong to a large number of groups, each pursuing different
ends. Some of these associations will be formally organised,
others will be traditional, informal groups governed, like the
family, by custom rather than by written regulations. Some
will pursue ends which are limited and specific, others will
have a purpose which is much wider and less easily specifi-
able. The English pluralists did not envisage these divisions
reinforcing each other, but thought of them as cutting across

one another, so that within a given state people of different races would join together in pursuing the same sport, and people of different religious persuasion would belong to the same trade unions. These theorists would have accepted T. S. Eliot's judgment that 'numerous cross-divisions favour peace within a nation, by dispersing and confusing animosities'.[16] A somewhat similar position has been defended by a number of American writers of recent years.

There will certainly be occasions on which individuals will find themselves torn between loyalty to one group and loyalty to another. There will inevitably be friction in a pluralist state. The individual will have to make up his mind what he should do in these cases of conflict. Perhaps the state will itself intervene, and side with one group against another on the particular issue; normally citizens will accept the decision of the state, because they accept the importance of there being some generally recognised machinery for maintaining order. But they may on a particular occasion refuse to accept the ruling of the state, and disobey, or even take to arms. Sometimes the state will go beyond its role as the mediator, and will attempt to pursue some national goal which it will impose upon its citizens. It will speak of a 'common good', or a 'general will', or a 'public interest', which is an all-embracing, substantive purpose to be followed by the state as a whole. In this case the state will sooner or later come into conflict with a number of the voluntary groups which are to be found within it. Forward-looking politicians dedicated to national objectives will anticipate the kind of conflicts which will arise, and will set about undermining the position of voluntary groups in the state. These groups will be called 'divisive', and their very right to exist will be challenged; they destroy the unity and coherence of the state. Discussing the means of preserving a tyranny, Aristotle wrote:

> One of them is the forbidding of common meals, clubs, education and anything of a like character. . . . A second measure is to prohibit societies for cultural purposes, and any gathering of a similar character; in a word, the adoption of every means for making every subject as much of a stranger as is possible to every other.[17]

The English pluralist writers believed that individual freedom is most likely to be preserved when a large number of associations exist within the state, and when the state does not itself pursue some national policy which purports to realise a common good. The state should concern itself with maintaining order and peace, by settling disputes between individuals and groups; so far as there is a common good worth considering, it is structural rather than substantive in nature. There will assuredly be tension and even friction between the groups, but this is not a wholly regrettable thing; in an imperfect world, freedom is more likely to survive in such a situation of friction. Furthermore it is in the context of conflicting claims made upon his loyalty that the individual develops his conscience and his personality. Pluralist writers disliked coercive authority, and believed that men should be encouraged to form self-governing associations to pursue the ends which they think valuable, rather than waiting for governments to act. They agreed with Proudhon that government is at best a necessary evil. 'To be governed', wrote Proudhon,

> is to be kept in sight, inspected, spied on, directed, law driven, numbered, enrolled, indoctrinated, preached at, controlled, estimated, assessed, censored, ordered about, by creatures who have neither the right, nor the wisdom nor the virtue to do so.[18]

Political pluralism, then, emerged at a time when the state was becoming increasingly active and powerful. Politicians frequently made claims which were totalitarian in their consequences and the fashionable political theories of the day gave undue prominence to the role of the state. The pluralist emphasis upon the importance of groups within the state, and particularly upon the crucial role of small groups, was a protest on the one hand against individualism and on the other against idealism. It was a cardinal belief of the pluralists that individualism and collectivism were but two sides of a single coin. Individualism, which was based upon a false view of human nature and of human relationships, led by easy stages to collectivism and to statism. Deny the political importance of the social life of citizens as it manifests itself in the family, the church, the sporting or cultural group, the civic association, and one is left with politics as a matter of 'the man versus the state'. Idealists, while they often recognised the importance of the role which groups play in the life of the individual, usually failed to carry these convictions into their political theories. They became either sponsors of state paternalism (often unwittingly), or of the ideology of 'self-help' along the lines recommended by the Charity Organisation Society.

In this volume we shall be concerned with the ideas of English political pluralists who wrote in the early decades of the present century. John Neville Figgis (1866-1919) is in many ways the most interesting and least understood of these writers, and a consideration of his political ideas will be a central concern of the book. Figgis's theory of the state was, however, strongly influenced by a number of earlier writers, in particular by Otto von Gierke (1844-1921), F. W. Maitland (1850-1906) and Lord Acton (1834-1902). Figgis helped Maitland to translate part of Gierke's great work *Das deutsche Genossenschaftsrecht*, which was published in 1900 under the title *Political Theories of the Middle Age*. From these two legal historians Figgis derived his notion of group personality. Acton was his colleague at Cambridge. Together with R. V. Laurence, Figgis later edited several volumes of Acton's letters and essays. Acton's almost fanatical belief in liberty infected his younger colleague, and this belief lies at the very foundation of Figgis's political pluralism. I shall also discuss the ideas of Harold J. Laski (1893-1950), G. D. H. Cole (1889-1959), Bertrand Russell (1872-1970) and other writers who shared pluralist ideas. As we shall see, these writers did not always agree with each other, but I shall suggest that their pluralist theories share a number of common features.[19]

Political pluralism was built upon a foundation of three pillars: (a) an insistence that 'liberty is the most important political value, and that it is best achieved in a state where power is distributed and dispersed, rather than being concentrated at one point; (b) a rejection of the idea of sovereignty; legal, political and moral; and (c) a notion of the real personality of groups. One chapter will be devoted to each of these themes. I shall then outline the positive theories of the pluralists about the relationship between the individual, the group and the state. An accusation which is frequently levelled against pluralism is that the group can be quite as oppressive to the individual as can the state. In the sixth chapter I shall consider the question of authority within groups, and look particularly at Figgis's ideas about authority in the church. Another chapter will deal with certain institutional consequences of pluralism, examining first the concept of a secular state, and then briefly mentioning other attempts which have been made to implement pluralist theories. In conclusion I shall discuss briefly the relationship between the theories of the English political pluralists and other concepts of pluralism.

2 Liberty and the Division of Power

The proper ends of political action are not self-evident. If there is one thing that a history of political thinking should teach us it is this: that there has been no generally agreed conclusion about what are the proper concerns of government. Some writers insist that the achievement of some kind of 'just' society is the end. Others claim that the state should be concerned with happiness; some think that equality must be achieved at all costs. Others again maintain that so long as life is protected and order is maintained, a government may do as it will; or put in contemporary (rather than in Hobbist) jargon, governments should be concerned with conflict resolution. Each of these positions may be criticised, but I shall simply make a few comments on the last-mentioned theory. Certainly major conflicts must be resolved, or contained, if a state is to continue; and it is clear that one of the jobs which a government must do is control conflicts in a state But conflicts can often be resolved in a number of different ways. Totalitarian governments achieve this aim in one way, while liberal governments attempt to do so in a somewhat different manner. Governments can attempt to resolve (or rather prevent) conflicts by suppressing subordinate groups. Duvalier remained in power for twice as long as many American presidents, and resolved conflicts in Haiti during that period. But the method he chose to accomplish this purpose is not the only method open to politicians; there are other ways of going about things, and we need to have some idea of which method is best — if not the absolute best, then the best in the circumstances. Moral debate cannot therefore be avoided.

Many political thinkers write as though the end which they happen to espouse is self-evidently the only possible end of politics. They thus seek to purge political theory of any ethical content; we do not, they argue, need to justify, to give reasons for, or to defend, our view about the duties of government. Bernard Crick goes so far as to *define* 'politics' as the conducting of the affairs of government in a manner of which he approves. Politics, he writes, 'can be simply defined as the activity by which differing interests within a given unit of rule are conciliated by giving them a share in power in proportion to their importance to the welfare and the survival of the whole community'.[1] Nevertheless, the very title of Crick's book, *In Defence of Politics*, recognises that if politics is defined in this way then the significant moral discussion is shifted to a defence of politics itself: why should we conduct the affairs of state in a *political* manner, rather than in any other manner? It is thus clear that Crick is not attempting to rid political theory of an ethical component.

Some writers claim that there are a number of values which a government should hold while conducting the affairs of state, and that it is impossible to reduce these to a single principle. Equality, freedom, justice, happiness, order, are all goods and need not be reduced to a single end. Although we may not reduce all political goods to a single principle, it certainly helps conduct if we are able to arrange our goods according to some kind of priority. For unless we have some hierarchy of goods we might get into difficulties deciding what we ought to do when potential goods conflict.

Even those, like Karl Popper, who hold that it is more important to eliminate evil in society than to achieve the good, must have some ideas about what is evil, and must be willing to defend their position in *moral* argument. Popper, of course, maintains that pain is the principal political evil which must be attacked by governments, and would seem to recognise that his difference with his critics on this matter is essentially a moral difference.

Closely connected to the idea that there are a number of political values none of which take priority over the others is the doctrine that there can be no such thing as a single *right* course of action for the individual in any context. There are, it is suggested, a number of 'goods' corresponding to the various roles which the individual plays in society, but there is no single course of right action in a given situation. If I am Prime Minister, I may come to the conclusion that what is good for me as a husband, or as a property owner, conflicts with what is good for me as a statesman, and there is no satisfactory way of resolving the conflict. I have simply to select one of the goods or to work out what is essentially an amoral compromise, and to act accordingly. This ethical pluralism, as it may be called, is closely connected to a particular sociological theory about the relation of the person to society. This theory is conveniently summarised by Walter Lippmann:

> the life of a modern man is not so much the history of a single soul; it is rather a play of many characters within a single body. . . . The modern man is unable any longer to think of himself as a single personality approaching an everlasting judgment.[2]

The notion has enjoyed considerable popularity among certain post-war American sociologists.[3] There can, according to this theory, be no course of right action for the individual person, as such an individual does not really exist as a moral being. There is a plurality of goods for the individual which are incommensurate. This is argued in two articles by S. P. Lamprecht. For him, there is a plurality of ends and there is 'neither one unified *summum bonum*, nor one single course of right conduct'. Not only does this writer say that there are several goods, which few would deny, but that 'there is a plurality of right conduct'.[4] The reason he gives for this latter assertion is that, as 'right' means aiming at the good and as there are several goods, there are thus several rights; which only shows that if you use words in an odd enough way you can prove almost anything. Surely by 'right' we normally mean that which ought to be done in any given situation. 'In the recognition of conduct as "right" ', observed Sidgwick,

> is involved an authoritative prescription to do it: but when we have judged conduct to be good, it is not yet clear that we ought to prefer this kind of good to all other good things.[5]

In an effort to show that there is no single right course of action in any situation, Lamprecht presents the reader with a difficult moral problem, regarding the number of soldiers a commander should sacrifice for the safety of a cathedral in wartime. This is rather like presenting us with a difficult mathematical problem as proof that there is no solution. 'The practical difficulties in the application of a rule', observed Walter Bagehot, 'do not disprove its being the true and the only one'.[6] The fact is that commanders have to take some course of action, and have to do so on the basis of some idea of right and wrong. According to the view of Lamprecht all we can hope for in politics is a kind of amoral compromise between the various possible goods in a situation. There is something of the same element of ethical pluralism in the thinking of A. F. Bentley. 'When we have reduced the legislative process to the play of group interests,' he wrote, 'then log-rolling, or give and take, appears as the very nature of the process. It is compromise, not in the abstract moral form, which philosophers can sagely discuss, but in the practical form with which every legislator who gets results through government is acquainted'.[7] While compromise is certainly an important aspect of politics, it is surely not the beginning and the end, as Bentley seems to assume. If half the population wishes to exterminate all the Jews and the other half wishes them to be left alone, how (if they have no belief in right action, but merely in amoral compromise) are these ethical pluralists to decide whether to kill half the Jews or half kill all the Jews? This is, to say the least, an unsatisfactory theory of ethics and politics and it is one with which the political pluralists with whom we are dealing in this monograph would have had little sympathy. They rejected the 'role' theory of the individual and insisted that there is such a thing as 'right conduct' in politics.

The principal English political pluralists insisted that the ends of politics must be ethically determined, and rejected the notion of the ethical pluralists that there can be no single right course of action in any situation. They insisted that the maximisation of liberty in society should be the principal end of political activity. Lord Acton's devotion to liberty is well known; much of his life was spent in collecting material for a projected history of liberty — 'the greatest book that was never written'. Acton insisted that liberty, or freedom (and I shall throughout use the terms synonymously), is the highest political end, and that the important thing to discover is not what a government does but what it allows to be done. Figgis also believed that it is the prime duty of a government to ensure as much freedom as possible in society, maintaining that it is upon liberty that all the minor ends of the state depend for their stability. Figgis asserted that freedom is good because it enables people to develop their personalities to the fullest extent. 'The theory of liberty', he wrote, 'is always concerned at bottom with human character.'[8] For Harold Laski, too, 'the emphasis upon freedom is made because it is believed that only in such fashion can the ethical significance of personality obtain its due recognition'.[9] The pluralist writers would have agreed with Gladstone that it is liberty alone which fits men for liberty; by being treated responsibly people develop a fuller sense of responsibility. All true liberals, Figgis insisted, must value human character above the efficiency of the state machinery. It is because the state is interested in human character that it should not attempt to mould character directly. A solid liberalism consists, according to these pluralist writers, in two propositions, (a) that the state ought to be concerned with the development of the personality of its citizens, and (b) that this personality develops best (as a general rule) when citizens are left as much choice as possible in determining how they should live their lives. If the first proposition were held without the second, the most extreme form of totalitarian paternalism might be justified. If the first proposition is denied, then the kind of liberalism which might be advocated would lack a solid basis.

Many writers have attempted to found liberalism on a sceptical basis, arguing that moral justifications of liberty are unnecessary. The Hobbes-Hume tradition of sceptical liberalism insists on seeing liberty as a residuum which governments may find it convenient to leave untouched by legislation. Although a wise government will avoid excessive meddling with the personal affairs of its citizens, there can be no claim on the part of the citizens to freedom as a right. While Figgis and Laski insisted that governments have a moral

duty to maintain the kind of peace and order in which as
much freedom of choice is left to as many people as possible,
the sceptics recognise no such moral duty; they therefore
deny that citizens have a right to as much freedom as is
possible in the situation. Certainly the pluralists acknowledged that there cannot be an absolute right to the same
amount of freedom in all contexts. In a state of siege or
during a war there can rarely be as much freedom as in
peacetime. Nevertheless it is still the duty of governments to
maximise freedom within a context of peace and order.
Limitations on freedom can ultimately be justified only by
the claim that a greater freedom is guaranteed by the restriction than would exist without the restriction. How can this
be? Surely restriction is the very opposite of freedom; the
more restrictions one has in a state the less freedom there is.
How is it possible then to say that restrictions can *increase*
freedom? Bentham had asked a similar question — surely
liberalism necessarily implies *laissez faire*. In his curious
book, *Fear of Power*, Preston King makes the same point.
Although it may in certain circumstances be right to confine
a man in prison, 'it seems something of an exaggeration to
argue that such acts promote "freedom" '.[10] With Bentham,
King agrees that the imprisonment may be justified, but on
grounds other than the maximisation of freedom. Bentham
admitted that although laws are an infraction of liberty, and
therefore an evil, they may be justified in so far as they
prevent a greater evil — in so far, that is, as they minimise
pain. He does not seem to conceive of the possibility of laws
increasing freedom in any way. Now although it is clearly
false to suggest that the freedom of the man imprisoned is
promoted by the action, it may very well be the case that the
freedom of others (whom *he* had been restricting) is promoted by confining the man. As L. T. Hobhouse put it:
freedom involves constraint, but it is constraint on something
else, 'that which is free being in the respect in which it is free
necessarily unconstrained'.[11] One would have thought that
King, from the nature of his argument, would have been the
first to agree that agencies other than the state may deprive
people of liberty, and that the state, therefore, in restricting
the activities of these agencies may increase the total freedom

in a society. Yet he thinks otherwise: 'Where one assumes liberty (*qua* autonomy) to be an absolute or ideal good, one can only accept (in consequence) the legitimacy of very little or of no government at all — barring doubletalk.'[12] This would, however, be true only in the ideal situation when each person exercised his liberty in such a way as to be compatible with the activities of every other person. Otherwise some degree of authority will be necessary to keep in being a situation in which maximum freedom can be enjoyed by the bulk of the people. It is thus false to suggest that, in any situation other than the ideal, a belief in liberty as the chief end in politics implies the legitimacy of 'no government at all' (or of 'very little government' — how little? How does 'very little government' enter into the argument? If by 'very little' King means no more than is necessary to maintain an ordered and peaceful state in which freedom may meaning-fully be enjoyed, the dogmatic liberal will agree with him — but this might be quite a lot of government in certain circumstances).

The pluralist writers, then, clearly recognised that some freedoms must be curtailed by government action if freedom is to be maximised in a state. It may be appropriate to mention here that they rejected J. S. Mill's attempt to draw 'a circle around every individual'[13] within which the indivi-dual must be left free to act as he chooses. Mill's distinction between self-regarding and other-regarding acts was scorn-fully discarded as indicating a misunderstanding of the nature of society. 'Few persons', wrote A. D. Lindsay,

> would now endorse J. S. Mill's distinction between actions which concern only the individual who does them and actions which concern other people also, as though anything a man did, or thought, or was, could be without effect on his fellows.[14]

Figgis concurred; how could anyone seriously accept Mill's distinction between 'acts purely self-regarding and those which are not'?[15] Laski agreed.[16] If Mill's critics had bothered to read the essay *On Liberty* with the same care that Mill wrote it, this kind of grotesque misrepresentation might have been avoided. Mill explicitly recognised that *all* actions may affect other people directly or indirectly; when he used the expression 'conduct which affects only himself', Mill went on immediately to qualify this:

> when I say only himself, I mean directly, and in the first instance; for whatever affects himself, may affect others through himself.[17]

Unfortunately this kind of carelessness is occasionally found in the writings of many of the English political pluralists. Barker, too, criticised Mill as the prophet of an empty and abstract individual, but happily avoided the kind of misrepresentation which we have noted.

A more telling argument against the position of the dogmatic liberal would be to maintain that freedoms are incommensurate and that it is therefore impossible to argue that by restricting A and thus liberating B, C and D, one is increasing the total freedom in a state. There is, according to this objection, no meaning which can properly be attached to the term 'total freedom in a state'; there are only particular freedoms and it is impossible to reduce these to a single quantitative scale. There is clearly some force in this objection; an example will illustrate what I mean. Mr Jones is prevented by the law from the practice of his religion which involves performing certain noisy rites in the middle of the night, thus depriving the Smiths, the Browns and the Percivals of the freedom to sleep (i.e. they are now obliged to stay awake during the period of Mr Jones's exercises, whereas before they were free either to sleep or to stay awake). Nevertheless who is to say that the freedom of religious expression which Jones claims is not more valuable than the relatively trivial freedoms of his neighbours? The U.S. Supreme Court often seems to think that it is. If freedoms are not commensurate then it is certainly impossible to decide how governments should act by simply referring to a 'libertarian calculus'. There must be some idea of a difference in qualities of freedom, and therefore we must agree that there are significant political values other than freedom. There is hardly any case of freedom being extended to one group of people in a state which does not involve some deprivation of freedom, however trivial and indirect, for other members of that state. This argument against liberty being the only political value seems to be fairly conclusive, but most of the pluralist writers we are here considering did not claim that it was the only value.

A solid liberalism must rely upon some conception of human nature. Acton's insistence upon the inviolability of conscience is well known. It was, in his view, the development of an idea of conscience which marks the greatest step forward in the history of liberty. 'The Christian notion of conscience', he taught,

> imperatively demands a corresponding measure of personal liberty. The feeling of duty and responsibility to God is the only arbiter of a Christian's actions. With this no human authority can be permitted to interfere.[18]

Tolerance of error, he observed, is necessary for freedom, and this tolerance is hard to defend in cases of *manifest* error except by a belief in the inviolability of conscience. The doctrine of the sovereignty of conscience promoted toleration, and 'all liberty is founded upon a belief in its infallibility'.[19] Acton held this latter belief in a radical manner, which could have anarchic consequences. Although it may be true that the individual has an absolute duty to follow his conscience, it may not be the case that the political authority is obliged in all cases to permit individuals to do so. In situations when the conscientious actions of a man might have disastrous consequences for others, the state may surely restrain that man; often it may do so in such a way as not to compromise the erring conscience of the man concerned, such as when a magistrate over-rules the conscientious objections of a Jehovah's Witness to a blood transfusion for his sick child. The life of the child may be saved, while the conscience of the Jehovah's Witness is intact — as he never consented to the transfusion.

Figgis and Laski both agreed with Acton that a strong doctrine of conscience is a necessary part of a sound liberalism. Nevertheless there is a limit to the freedom which society can permit to anti-social consciences, particularly in times of emergency. They would rather have agreed with Mandell Creighton's remark that,

society cannot be altogether abolished to suit people's
consciences. But I am bored with people's consciences. Let
them be requested to leave off growing conscientious
scruples, and grow cauliflowers, or some other useful
product.[20]

Discussing the position of conscientious objectors in the
1914-18 war, Figgis wrote that in his judgment it was right
to assure liberty to genuine C.O.s; but owing to its obvious
abuse severe measures should be taken to test the reality of
the conviction. Yet he believed that it is the duty of the
individual to follow his conscience ultimately, after having
given due weight to the relevant authorities. Blind obedience
to any authority, however, leads to a corruption of the
conscience. Laski thought that J. H. Newman's discussion of
conscience in his *Letter to the Duke of Norfolk* was 'the
profoundest analysis of sovereignty the nineteenth century
produced'.[21] There Newman replied to Gladstone's claims
that owing to the Vatican Council's definition of papal infallibility a Roman Catholic could no longer be a loyal
citizen, and that the papal authority will always take prece-
dence over the claim of the civil government. Newman maintained that for the Roman Catholic the papacy is the
supreme ecclesiastical authority, but it is ultimately the conscience which recognises it as such:

> if either the Pope or the Queen demanded of me an
> 'Absolute Obedience', he or she would be transgressing the
> laws of human nature and human society. I give an abso-
> lute obedience to neither.[22]

Acton had insisted that the first agent in the development of
conscience must be religious or quasi-religious. Though christianity has not always been characterised by a belief in the
freedom of conscience, it was in a christian context that the
belief reached its fullest and most adequate expression. It was
the doctrine of conscience which brought over religion to the
cause of freedom. Figgis believed that the notion of freedom
is intimately connected to a belief in 'the spiritual nature of
men'.[23] The materialist doctrine that man is a complicated
machine hardly has a place for a high doctrine of conscience,

nor, therefore, for a solid conception of human freedom; why should too much fuss be made about civil liberty if the individual is simply a lump of matter moved here and there by a number of contending forces?

Laski agreed with Acton and Figgis that a strong doctrine of conscience is an indispensable underpinning for a sound liberalism, and regarded his pluralistic position as taking away from the state and giving back to the individual conscience that superior morality with which the former had wrongly been invested. He did not, however, base his politics on a religious foundation, but upon a humanist belief in the importance of individual personality. Bernard Zylstra concludes from his detailed study of Laski's political ideas that

> If there is a line of continuity in his thought from the very first of his publications to the end of his life, it should be sought in his insistence upon the central place of individual man.[24]

When the pluralist writers argued that liberty is one of the chief ends of political activity, did they think of liberty in the negative Hobbist sense of an absence of external impediments to action, or did they have a more positive notion of freedom? The pluralists we are considering were not philosophers and there is often, in their writings, a regrettable imprecision in the use of concepts. Acton defined freedom in various ways; he claimed that freedom is not the power of doing what we like, but 'the right of being able to do what we ought'.[25] This has definite traces of a rationalist notion of freedom, which pictures a man as free when he lives under the guidance of reason; though Acton here thought of a man as free when he is *able* to do as he ought (rather than when he is actually doing as he ought, which is the fully-fledged rationalist notion of freedom). In his later writings, however, Acton introduced a further subjective element. 'By liberty,' he declared in 1877, 'I mean the assurance that every man shall be protected in doing what he believes his duty. . . .'[26] Figgis recognised that there is a danger in speaking of freedom as the right to do as we ought; such a definition of freedom can easily lead to a justification of tyranny in terms of freedom.[27] Yet he seems to have put forward no satisfactory notion of freedom to take its place. Laski spoke of T. H. Green's concept of freedom as 'more valuable' than the negative empiricist position,[28] and wrote of liberty as 'the positive and equal opportunity of self-realisation'.[29] He even stated in one place that to compel obedience to 'rules of convenience which promote right living' is not to make a man unfree.[30] Most of the other pluralist writers were in roughly the same position, acknowledging the inadequacy of the negative Hobbist or Spencerian concept of freedom as 'absence of restraint', and yet failing to work out a satisfactorily coherent alternative.

It is difficult to find in the writings of G. D. H. Cole a consistent notion of freedom. In *Social Theory* (1920) he put forward the following analysis: freedom can, in the last resort, apply only to the individual person — but it can apply to him directly in the form of 'personal liberty', and indirectly in the form of 'social liberty'. By personal liberty Cole meant the negative empiricist conception of freedom as 'being let alone':

> it is simply the freedom of the individual to express without external hindrance his 'personality' — his likes and dislikes, desires and aversions, hopes and fears, his sense of right and wrong, beauty and ugliness.[31]

This, of course, is a definition with which neither Hobbes nor Spencer would wish to quarrel. Social liberty, on the other hand, is the freedom of groups — or to be more precise — the freedom of the individual in so far as he is a member of groups. This freedom has an internal and an external aspect. The latter is 'the freedom of the association from external dictation *in respect of its manner of performing its function*'.[32] He maintained that this external freedom 'implies' internal freedom, interpreted as the democratic organisation of the group itself. Why external freedom implies internal freedom he did not say; and it seems quite possible for a group to be free from external restraint and at the same time hierarchically or aristocratically governed within. Unfortunately, Cole also clouds the issue by trying to maintain that economic equality is implied in his notion of personal liberty.

It is definitely not clear how the idea of 'being let alone' involves the introduction of social and economic equality. Certainly private agencies — groups other than the government — may interfere with individual freedom (as we have already had occasion to observe); state action may be called for to prevent such interference, and be justified in terms of the maximising of freedom in society; but it is not at all clear how economic *equality* is demanded by the notion of freedom which Cole puts forward.

In an earlier book Cole vigorously attacked the rationalist notion of freedom,[33] though in the previous year he seems to have defended a concept of freedom very similar to the rationalist notion; he wrote as follows:

> Freedom is not simply the absence of restraint; it assumes a higher form when it becomes self-government. A man is not free in himself while he allows himself to remain at the mercy of every idle whim: he is free when he governs his own life according to a dominant purpose or system of purposes.[34]

Cole changed his position with every book he wrote and it is quite impossible to derive a coherent theory from these pluralist writings of his. Bertrand Russell, on the other hand, seems consistently to have assumed an empiricist notion of freedom. 'Liberty in itself is a negative principle,' he wrote, 'it tells us not to interfere, but does not give any basis for construction.'[35] He nevertheless rejected the kind of 'negative liberty' which had been advocated by Herbert Spencer, arguing that by giving freedom to the strong to suppress the weak we do not maximise freedom in a society; it is possible to increase the total freedom in a society by restricting the activities of a minority.[36]

Thus while they accepted liberty as one of the principal ends of politics most of the pluralist writers whom we are considering in this essay had not thought through the various complications in the notion of freedom. At times they used a definition of freedom which the most extreme empiricist could accept; while elsewhere they scornfully rejected the empiricist idea of freedom as unsatisfactory. They recognised that liberty must be limited by law if a state is to be maintained in which there is some semblance of order, insisting that unless such order be established, no freedom can meaningfully be possessed by the members of that society. The notion of freedom which they generally assumed was more than 'being let alone'; a man, to be free to do something, must have the means or the power to do it. And this implies a society in which there is order and some approximation to social justice and economic equality.

The Corrupting Influence of Power is the English title of a book by Gerhart Ritter, and sums up in a phrase an essential aspect of pluralist thought. Lord Acton, whose dictum on the corrupting tendency of power is frequently quoted (and more frequently misquoted), had a considerable influence on the ideas of the English political pluralists. If we are to understand the pluralist movement properly we must see it as an adaptation to the conditions of the early twentieth century of the traditional whig distrust of power. This suspicion of power and demand for constitutional safeguards, virile groups and general decentralisation are traditional whig ideas, and the pluralist movement might be seen as a legitimate development of these earlier whig notions. The separation of power is, for the whig, an essential prerequisite of a liberal society; this separation can be achieved in several ways. The whig was, during the nineteenth century, fighting a losing battle and often appears to have been a mere conservative; yet it would be a mistake to think that writers like Tocqueville were essentially conservative. Tocqueville was not averse from change in itself, but from change which abolished local powers and group loyalties in favour of a centralised system of organisation. Centralisation, he argued, was already taking place during the *ancien régime*, but without the great success which accompanied it after the revolution. Before the revolution there were many old, and in themselves vicious, institutions which acted as breakwaters, albeit irregular and ill-constructed, against the omnipotence of the central power. The centralising tendencies of the old regime were best seen in the French administration of Canada and Algeria, where they could be operated unhindered by traditional vested interests. Some social power must, he held, predominate over other groups, but if this is unchecked it becomes dangerous;

unlimited power is bad. Whereas a strong centralised administration can achieve great things in a short time, once it does break down, the whole of society falls apart. 'When power is dispersed,' on the other hand, 'action is clearly hindered, but there is strength elsewhere'.[37] He saw the discussions on the new French constitution of 1851 as concerned primarily with the question of the limitation of power. One thing which the French could not establish, he pointed out, is a free government, and the one thing which they could not get rid of is centralisation. Napoleon had speeded up the centralising tendency of the *ancien régime*, while the restoration and the government of July were as absolute centralisers as Napoleon himself.

If Tocqueville can be said to represent the right-wing revolt against the concentration of power, Proudhon played a similar role on the left wing. He endeavoured to combat (as did the guild socialists in a later age) the centralising tendency of socialism; centralism is, he declared, incompatible with liberty. He divided regimes into two sorts, authoritarian and liberal; the essential characteristic of the former is the concentration of power, while the latter are distinguished by a division of power. Centralisation not merely endangers the liberty of individuals and associations, but is not particularly efficient. '*Avec la centralisation*', Lamennais had declared, '*vous avez l'apoplexie au centre et la paralysie aux extrémités.*'[38]

It was this aspect of the thought of St Thomas Aquinas that led Lord Acton to call him the first whig. 'My view,' he wrote in a letter to Figgis,

> is that the revolutionary doctrine goes back to St. Thomas, and it is he, and not the evil one, that I call the First Whig.[39]

In a lecture on the political ideas of Aquinas, Figgis tried to show what Acton had meant by the statement. First of all, the whig regards freedom as the true end of politics,

> To this was added the sense, that freedom can only be secured by a careful distribution of power among different bodies checking each other.[40]

Acton declared that the puritans of the seventeenth century believed that the sphere of government should be limited and that this would be achieved by a division of power. Others, however, like Carlyle and Froude believed the opposite doctrine; 'They hold,' wrote Acton,

> that great and salutary things are done for mankind by power concentrated, not by power balanced and cancelled and dispersed, and that the whig theory, sprung from decomposing sects, the theory that authority is legitimate only by virtue of its checks, and that the sovereign is dependent on the subject, is rebellion against the divine will manifested all down the stream of time.[41]

The Middle Ages were seen as the period in which power was dispersed, and in which many semi-autonomous groups flourished; absolute power was thought to be more intolerable than slavery. Yet Marsilius had sounded the trumpet of a new movement; with him, Figgis pointed out, there is almost no feudalism, no use of the system of estates which led to whiggery.

> nor is there any of that system of checks and balances which are the result of medieval life, and preserve freedom at the expense of efficiency — no it is the omnicompetent, universal, all absorbing modern State, the mortal God, the great Leviathan of later teachers . . . not power divided, but power concentrated and united.[42]

With the renaissance came a concentration of power; in Venice, Acton lamented, power passed from the nobility to a committee, from the committee to a council of ten, from the ten to three Inquisitors in which form by 1600 it had become 'a frightful despotism'.[43] Yet there was a tradition of whiggery which carried through from Aquinas and the early Jesuit writers to Locke and Sidney. Richard Niebuhr has pointed out how the American puritans were similarly suspicious of power.[44] Acton's own position was clear. 'Suspect power more than vice,' he advised his history students at Cambridge.[45] The possession of unlimited power not only corrupts the people over whom power is exercised, but 'corrodes the conscience, hardens the heart, and confounds the understanding of monarchs'.[46] 'Liberty', he informed Mary Gladstone, 'depends on the division of power,'[47] and he quoted with approval the dictum of Fénelon that power is poison.

This administrative centralisation and concentration of power had continued throughout the nineteenth century; 'Some would warn us,' Maitland observed in 1900,

> that in the future the less we say about a supralegal, suprajural plenitude of power concentrated in a single point at Westminster — concentrated in one single organ of an increasingly complex commonwealth — the better for that commonwealth may be the days that are coming.[48]

How then are we to remedy this danger of power? Since the 'demon' of power can never be destroyed, the task of mankind, it has been argued, 'is to clip its wings'.[49] Power, the pluralists believed, was in itself a great danger, and must be checked: all men are, in part at least, wicked, and any ruler with absolute power is likely to misuse it. There is, believed Laski, a poison in power against which nations must be on their guard;[50] he agreed with Tocqueville that by limiting power we limit the ability to do good, but we also limit the chance of doing evil. Pluralists would, on the whole, have concentrated on avoiding the worst in politics rather than on trying to achieve the best. They rejected the Hobbist notion that anarchy is the only great threat to society, and that absolute power must be put into the hands of the rulers in order to avert this danger; the preservation of life at any cost was not for them the sole end of politics. The pluralists were pessimistic with regard to individuals and optimistic with regard to the mass of men; they trusted man but distrusted men. Things will be better — freedom will be preserved — Laski insisted, if' we keep power from the few and spread it out among the many, dividing it 'upon the basis of the functions it is to perform'.[51] It is the concentration of power to which they objected, and they aimed not at educating the despot, but at preventing the accumulation of power. They would have agreed with Sorel's criticism of the socialists of his day: *'Ils attaquent plutôt les hommes au pouvoir que le pouvoir lui-même.*'[52] They did not claim that power is evil in itself, but that the evil results of power concentrated almost invariable outweighed the good consequences. By dividing power we encourage responsibility among men. Russell agreed, and further argued that by preventing the concentration of power in the hands of 'officials and captains of industry', we

> diminish the opportunities for acquiring the habit of command, out of which the desire for exercising tyranny is apt to spring. Strong organisations like trade unions, churches, cultural associations, are to be welcomed as safeguards of liberty.[53]

There are various ways of distributing power and many of these were advocated by the thinkers whom we have been discussing. Traditional groups should be preserved and must be regarded as bulwarks against the total state, while voluntary associations should also be encouraged. The totalitarian and the tyrant always aim at breaking down these groups and reducing their subjects to a mass of unassociated atoms; Aristotle knew this. Burke thought that the French had

> first destroyed all the balances and counterpoises which serve to fix the state, and to give it a steady direction . . . and then they melted down the whole into one incongruous, ill-connected mass.[54]

Traditional groups should be maintained, and constitutional checks upon the central power should be in operation. Tocqueville held the same opinion on despotism; it seeks to rid society of corporation, class and even of family ties, and isolates men from each other. In a new society, like America, based on the democratic principle, there are few traditional institutions to protect men from the invasions of the government, and the only remedy which he could see was the creation of voluntary associations and the preservation of a genuine federalism. In aristocratic societies there are a number of powerful individuals and families who can check the claims of the central government; it is the office of voluntary groups and artificially created political divisions to stand in lieu of these in democratic states.

During the nineteenth century a tradition of Roman Catholic political thought grew up which emphasised the importance of groups in society. Baron von Ketteler, the Bishop of Mainz, who was one of the leaders of this catholic social movement, pointed back to the middle ages when a mass of autonomous groups flourished and when 'concentrated unlimited power in the hands of a single man was unknown'.[55] The right of local and functional self-government was held to be essential for a truly free society. There was, he argued, a dangerous tendency abroad to break down societies into a mass of individuals; having done this the autocrat has less powerful opposition and can do practically what he likes.[56] By 1891 the pope was stating that there should be a right to form worker associations, while a later pope proclaimed that small groups should be allowed a maximum of self-government, and that large groups like the state should not arrogate to themselves functions which can be performed efficiently by smaller societies.

Lord Acton was keen that the freedom of groups should be maintained and increased. He told Simpson that what was most needed for a theory of liberty was a right notion of corporations, and their place in society. The modern theory, he lamented, condemned all groups beside the state as subversive, and recognises only an atomic freedom for the individual. In his essay on 'Nationality', Acton argued that many national groups within a state would check the tendency to absolutism. F. W. Maitland pointed in horror to France where,

> we may see the pulverising, macadamising tendency in all its glory, working from century to century, reducing to impotence, and then to nullity, all that intervenes between Man and State.[57]

Figgis even more perhaps than his masters saw the liberty of groups as the essential element in a free society. 'The battle of freedom in this century', he declared from the pulpit, 'is the battle of small societies to maintain their inherent life as against the all-devouring Leviathan of the whole'.[58] Small groups in particular must be allowed to take their place alongside the larger associations if freedom is to be a positive

thing. Toleration was achieved in England not by the mere
assertion of individual rights, but it was 'the religious body,
the sect with its passionate assertion of its own right to be,
which finally won toleration from the State'.[59]

There are, however, countries such as America where traditional barriers do not exist in great number; what is to be
done to secure liberty? The answer of the whig is federation.
By separating the executive from the legislature, and the state
governments from the federal government, the constitution
of the United States enabled a free society to remain in
existence. Acton regarded the distribution of power among
several states as the best check upon popular democracy, and
a large democratic state cannot maintain the principle of
self-government but by federalism of some sort. Tocqueville
saw the separation of power among the states of the union as
a guarantee against absolutism. Proudhon too regarded the
federal system as essentially opposed to centralised absolutism. As against the authoritative or monarchical principle,
which had as its accompaniments the elimination of group
loyalties, the concentration of power and a feudal economy,
Proudhon set the federal system, which carried with it local
self-government, the separation of power and an agricultural-
industrial federation. The pluralist movement can be regarded
as an aspect of federalism, and it has been argued that 'The
greatest contribution to the federal idea in Great Britain is,
without doubt, the rise of the pluralist theory of the state.'[60]
Figgis spoke of the medieval principle behind the House of
Commons as a 'semi-federalist polity',[61] while the Council of
Constance 'stands for an inchoate federalism . . . as against a
centralising bureaucracy.'[62]

It is therefore the case that the pluralist writers are the
inheritors of a long tradition, which feared the concentration
of power and sought to build and maintain strong barriers to
stem its force; these barriers might be found in traditional
groups and aristocracies, in voluntary associations, in national
groups or in federal constitutions, but the purpose is always
the same. It is perhaps true, however, that the pluralists failed
to see the possible danger of strong groups; it is quite as
conceivable for individual freedom to be infringed by group
action as by the action of the state, and thinkers of this

persuasion must always be on their guard against the possibility of group tyranny. To say that they ignored this potential danger of group tyranny would be wrong, and, as we shall see, many of them insisted on the necessity of a strong state above the groups to control them, yet it may be true that they were not sufficiently alive to the danger.

Thus, not only was it held by the pluralists to be the case that true freedom implies a recognition of the life of groups in a state, but also that the existence of groups helps to ensure freedom of thought and action for the individual. 'Liberty provokes diversity,' Acton pointed out, 'and diversity preserves liberty by supplying the means of organisation'.[63] That fact was used by Figgis to explain the rise of toleration in England. 'Political liberty', Figgis declared in a famous phrase, 'is the fruit of ecclesiastical animosities.'[64] It was the claim of religious bodies to freedom of speech and worship which led to the tolerant state which we know today. The reformers were by no means in favour of religious liberty, and the reformation so far from checking, actually developed and encouraged 'the orgy of State-autocracy which set in with the Renaissance'.[65] Only indirectly can we ascribe the development of toleration to the reformation — it stimulated the growth of religious groups, the struggle between which was to bring some measure of toleration, and freedom.[66] Also, as Creighton had said, it is a great mistake to think that the English puritans were essentially in favour of religious liberty; they were willing to allow freedom only to those with whom they were in general agreement. 'Political liberty, *as such*', observed Figgis, 'never was and never will be an ideal of Puritanism'.[67] Nor was toleration the result of religious indifference, as is sometimes suggested,[68] much more is it true to say that religious indifference is the result of toleration.

Toleration, then, was not achieved by any single group, but by the failure of any group to predominate sufficiently to crush the rest; toleration was thrust upon us. It was, according to Acton, to the clash between the church and the state in the middle ages — or more accurately to the struggle between *regnum* and *sacerdotium* — that we owe the rise of

religious liberty; in a society where church and state are
united under one head, as in England, there is a danger of this
liberty disappearing. The gradual growth of religious sects,
however, and the clash which took place between them and
the established church, replaced the medieval dichotomy and
led to a policy of religious toleration. Hardly any of these
bodies valued liberty in itself, and, as Figgis pointed out,

> The two religious bodies which have done the most to
> secure 'the rights of man' are those two which really cared
> least about individual liberty, and made the largest inroads
> upon private life wherever they obtained the supremacy —
> the Roman Catholic Church and the Presbyterian.[69]

Neither Bellarmine nor Knox would wish to be regarded as
the herald or instrument of the tolerant state, but such they
were. It was not primarily the claim of individuals to freedom
of speech which led to toleration, but the claim of groups to
freedom of assembly. 'By himself apart from religious dis-
cords the individual would have secured no freedom.'[70]

Few, then, believed in liberty as a political end. Figgis
mentioned the Benthamites and Hoadly; Acton added Soci-
nus, the independent founders of Rhode Island and the
Quaker patriarch of Pennsylvania — these dogmatic liberals
were the true prophets of liberty. Things began to change
though, and as Butterfield reminds us, toleration which had
been a political necessity was turned into a religious ideal.
Yet as late as 1893 Creighton could declare, in his essay on
Persecution and Tolerance, that too often we were tolerant
only because it happened to suit us to be so. But if religious
liberty has come about almost by accident, we must, Creighton held, defend it dogmatically as the right thing. We have
seen how Figgis was eager that liberty should be defended as
a dogma rather than as a mere expedient, and how he
regarded the tolerant society as the best society.

Bearing all this in mind, it is not at all easy to see what
Harold Laski meant when in his post-pluralist period he
criticised Figgis for failing to recognise clearly that,

> (i) the concessions were always grudging because some
> religious group or other remained dominant and a religious

group is *more suo* exclusive, (ii) that the concessionaire didn't care a damn about freedom for any of its rivals and, the Quakers apart, would probably have persecuted if it could.[71]

Figgis had made his position quite clear on this historical issue and it is astonishing that Laski was able to misrepresent him in this manner. 'This achievement of individual liberty,' Figgis had written,

> was never attained and except for the short period of the Benthamite movement never sought merely for its own sake. Its achievement became feasible only because it was connected with the recognition of the right to exist of some society usually religious, which the civil magistrate did not desire to exist. It is often agreed that religious differences are the ground of modern liberty. It is a mistake to suppose . . . that this is because as a rule any or all religious bodies cared about such liberty. What they desired was the right to be, what they denied was the right of the State to suppress them as societies.[72]

Liberty and toleration in England have, Figgis taught, come about principally through the struggle of religious groups to live. Virile groups will always provide a bulwark against statism and are to be encouraged by liberals. Yet a group can easily become too powerful and tyrannise over other groups and individuals. A strong state is needed which will be above the groups, whose purpose is to keep them within the bounds of peace and justice.

3 The Attack on Sovereignty

The theory of political pluralism rests upon three pillars; the second is the denial of state sovereignty, in almost any sense which that term can have. Before outlining the nature of the pluralist attack upon state sovereignty it is necessary to draw some important distinctions. This clarification will be attempted by outlining the development of the idea of sovereignty during the nineteenth century — particularly in the British context. Unfortunately it will be necessary to traverse what James Bryce called, the 'dusty desert of abstractions through which successive generations of political philosophers have thought it necessary to lead their disciples'.[1] I shall begin by stating the theory of John Austin, and consider the modifications which were introduced into it by A. V. Dicey, D. G. Ritchie and James Bryce.

I

An independent political society, for Austin, is a society in which there is a determinate person or body of persons which, while not obeying habitually the will of another, itself is habitually obeyed by the bulk of the people. This body is the sovereign. It should be emphasised that Austin did not believe that this body is always obeyed by all the people. Laws are the commands of this body which is 'incapable of *legal* limitation', and is thus 'legally *despotic*'.[2] The body which is habitually obeyed is not entirely free from limitation, either political or moral; it must consult the opinions of the people, and is limited by positive morality and by the law of God. He thought that the sovereign in Britain was the Monarch, the House of Lords and the House of Commons, or, 'speaking accurately', the electors of the Commons. Thus there was, for Austin, one sovereign, who was, while in the legal sense unlimited, in the political and moral sphere limited by public opinion, positive morality and the law of God. In Britain the power which is habitually obeyed by the bulk of the people is Parliament (with the proviso that at the time of an election the persons enfranchised take up active participation in sovereignty); this body is legally unlimited.

Austin suffered much criticism at the end of the nineteenth century. Sir Henry Maine informed the world that the assertion that in any society 'the irresistible force' was stored up in one man or body of men was not so much false as 'only verbally true', and went on to point out that,

> the vast mass of influences, which we may call for shortness moral, perpetually shapes, limits or forbids the actual direction of the forces of society by its Sovereign.[3]

But Austin never denied this.

Then a distinction was drawn between the legal and the political sovereign. A. V. Dicey declared that, in England, Parliament is sovereign legally, and that there is no legal appeal from its commands. On the other hand the political sovereign, 'the will of which is ultimately obeyed by the citizens of the state', is, 'in strict accuracy', the body of electors, whose will 'is sure ultimately to prevail on all subjects to be determined by the British Government'.[4] D. G. Ritchie distinguished, in addition to the legal and political sovereigns, a nominal sovereign, in whose name executive acts are performed, and this is the Monarch in Britain. The legal sovereign must be a definite body or thing and is 'the authority behind which the lawyer *qua* lawyer will not and cannot go'.[5] With regard to a political sovereign, Ritchie believed that there is in any society a 'power which is ultimate', although this does not reside in any person or body. James Bryce accepted this distinction between legal and political sovereignty. In addition to the legal sovereign,

> There is in every State a Strongest Force, a power to which other powers bow, and of which it may be, more or less positively predicted that in case of conflict it will overcome all resistance.[6]

The residing place of this force is the political (or, as he calls it, 'practical') sovereign. Later, however, he tells the reader that the practical sovereign does not enjoy 'utterly uncontrolled power'.[7] The essence of this criticism of Austin is that there are two sovereignties, the political and legal. While the latter is conceived to be in the hands of a definite person or body of persons, the former is in the control of 'the electors', or 'public opinion'.[8] If we were to ask Dicey, Ritchie and Bryce to be more specific, they would, I think, refuse to help us. In the thought of Ritchie, the only way to specify this 'power' which will ultimately prevail is to see what *does* ultimately prevail; it is in the hands of no determinate person or body. Ritchie tells us nothing about the political sovereign except that it is the (indeterminate) body which controls the power which ultimately prevails in a dispute. As there is no such thing as a power which prevails in social disputes, but a situation which results, the whole concept of political sovereignty is somewhat vacuous. Dissatisfied with the obvious inadequacy of the Austinian notion, these thinkers have so widened the concept of sovereignty as to make it meaningless. Instead of telling us, as Ritchie at first appears to, that there is a body that exists somewhere which we can, perhaps, consult, and whose will always prevails, he merely says that 'whatever will be will be', and invents a fictitious thing — a political sovereign — which is thought to have willed the situation which prevails. The same might be said of Dicey, though he appears to be more specific, when he declares the 'electors' to be sovereign. Does he mean the majority of the electors? If so, he is wrong; it is quite possible to conceive of a situation in which a minority of the electors with the support of troops and police could hold down the majority. If he becomes evasive, and says that it is difficult to know what the electors will on a particular occasion until after the event, then his statement that the will of the electors ultimately prevails, is perilously near to a tautology.[9] We may agree with Henry Sidgwick's typically restrained comment, that the effort of Dicey and others to put forward a theory of a political sovereign divorced from the legal sovereign 'seems to me highly dubious'.[10]

W. J. Rees tried some years ago[11] to rehabilitate the

notion of what I have called a political sovereign; he distinguished two kinds of political sovereign: a coercive and an influential sovereign. He further divided the former into an institutionally coercive sovereign, and a socially coercive sovereign. Rees's whole essay is characterised by a somewhat barren conceptualism, and little attempt is made to apply the concepts which he distinguishes to the realities of political life. His question 'Where is the influential sovereign located?' betrays a serious misunderstanding of the nature of political decision-making. We are rarely, if ever, able to point to one person or body of persons whose actions by themselves determine a particular decision. Decisions are made in the context of a number of different groups and individuals each attempting to bring various pressures and influences to bear on the situation, including at times the threat or actual use of force. The alliances between the associations themselves, and between individuals, are usually shifting, and will change as the issue to be decided changes. It is obviously the case that some groups will have more influence or more power than others, but there is probably no country where a single identifiable group is able unilaternally to determine all political decisions, without reference to the interests and opinions of other groups.

There is however, another sort of sovereignty which we cannot ignore. This is what may be called 'moral sovereignty' — the claim that there is in the state an authority to which obedience is due whatever it wills, a body whose commands are morally binding in all circumstances. This conception of sovereignty distinguishes Austin (who rejected it) from Hobbes and from Green (who accepted it, though in different senses). A man can be obliged to do something, so the theory runs, only if he has in some way willed it himself. For Hobbes, men desire order above everything except life itself, and so long as the sovereign keeps order and protects life, the citizens are morally obliged to obey him. This obligation proceeds not from fear, but from a promise to obey (though fear is, of course, among the most significant psychological causes for persons making and keeping the promise, and is therefore vital in making the promise an effective act). There is, insisted Hobbes, 'no obligation on any man, which ariseth

not from some act of his own'.[12] The moral sovereignty of
Leviathan stems from the consent or promise of the citizens
— this can, for Hobbes, be the only possible source of its
authority. Kant also believed that an action can be a duty for
me only if it is in accordance with a principle to which I
consent — a principle which is self-imposed. A person, Kant
maintained, 'is bound only to act in conformity with a will
which is his own'.[13] Rousseau too insisted that a form of
society must be evolved in which each man obeys himself
alone; he developed the notion of a general will which always
wills the common good, and therefore represents the real will
of all citizens. Thus when a man is forced to do something
which he does not want to do, he is being helped to do what
he *really* wills. T. H. Green believed that Rousseau's concept
of a general will distinguished him from all previous political
thinkers, and constituted his great contribution to political
theory. The true sovereign, according to Green, embodies the
general will, which is my will, and the citizen is thus obliged
to obey the state (in so far as the actual state approaches the
idea) because he has willed (perhaps unconsciously) the laws
which it commands. Moral obligation, Green asserted, must
be self-imposed and the laws of a state are binding only
because they are thought to have been willed by the subjects.
Will, rather than force, is the basis of the state. Thus by a
fiction of consent, made plausible through the distinction
between a real and an apparent will, a halo is placed above
the state, which is given an authority that is absolutely
binding upon the consciences of citizens. The fallacy that
duty can arise only from consent, thus unites thinkers as
different as Hobbes and Green, Kant and Rousseau. Although
certain writers try to draw liberal conclusions from this
theory, the natural consequence is authoritarian and potentially totalitarian, laying all the emphasis upon *who* commands and paying little attention to *what* is commanded.

A contemporary example of this type of political theory
can be seen in a little book by Joseph Tussman, *Obligation
and the Body Politic*. There he writes as follows:

'I have a duty to . . .' seems to follow from 'I have agreed
to' in a way that it does not follow from 'I am forced to'

or 'I am in the habit of'. This is sometimes expressed as the view that obligations are, or even must be, voluntarily assumed.[14]

It is not quite clear how Tussman believes that duty 'seems to follow from' a promise, but even if the relationship is as strong as implication (which it is not; if I promise to kill my parents today in a fit of rage, it is by no means clear that I have a duty to kill them tomorrow), this is very different from saying that obligations must voluntarily be assumed. He gives us no indication as to why obligations must voluntarily be assumed. Later in his essay he truly says that there is nothing inherently authoritative about a majority, but goes on to say that a minority are bound by the decision of the majority only if they 'consider the decision as *theirs*'.[15] Surely the minority is bound by the majority decision if it considers that decision to be right, or if it thinks that the mischief done by resisting would be greater than the mischief done by complying. Why must they consider the decision as 'theirs'?

How is it then that so many thinkers have believed that duty can arise only from promise or consent? It is certainly true that we can hardly *blame* a man for acting in a way which he believes to be right. We cannot condemn him for not acting in accordance with a rule that he does not recognise, for not following a law of right conduct which he does not accept. Nevertheless there is surely a distinction between recognising a rule of right conduct as binding upon me, and my promising to follow such a rule. I may believe that wanton cruelty is wrong without having consented or promised not to behave cruelly. Certainly promises create a *prima facie* obligation; but they are not a source of absolute obligation, nor are they the only source of obligations. I can therefore properly be blamed for an act only if I see it to be wrong — but I need not have promised or consented not to act in this way. We may, of course, want to go on to say that, although the person is not to be condemned or blamed for an action which he believes to be in accordance with a criterion of goodness which he accepts, the act (considered as an act) is wrong, owing to the fact that either (a) the criterion which he accepts is faulty, or (b) he is mistaken in believing that his particular act is in accordance with that criterion. On the utilitarian model, then, I could recognise, by reason, that the greatest happiness principle is binding upon me, without ever having promised or consented to behave in accordance with it. On the intuitionist model I could believe that something is right, by intuition, without having by an act of will promised in any way to do it.

II

Pluralist writers were critical of all these notions of sovereignty which we have distinguished above, legal, political and moral. They attacked the idea of the sovereign state from the standpoint of the doctrine of the inherent rights of groups which they had derived largely from Gierke. Figgis has been accused of misinterpreting Gierke, who is said to have been a believer in the sovereign state. By sovereignty, however, the German theorist meant something rather different from the English idea of sovereignty. He meant by sovereignty of the state, that the state should be subject to no superior human will. 'The state alone', he wrote,

> cannot be subordinate as sovereign collective person to any organised will-power external to and above it, and consequently it cannot be limited in its will and action by a higher community participating in its decisions.[16]

This does not, however, imply that the state is above law, which it creates (i.e. the state is not legal sovereign in the English sense). The state is, in Gierke's thought, morally as well as legally bound to recognise the rights and personality of groups and of individuals; it is thus not moral sovereign. Like his hero Althusius, Gierke saw the state as enshrining the general will in some of its manifestations, and what distinguishes the state from other groups is its possession of sovereign power.[17] Barker declares that Figgis's theory 'which runs counter to the idea of the unitary State' is 'alien to the logic' of Gierke's general position.[18] This is only partly true, and there is certainly a sense in which Gierke was a pluralist.[19] I shall discuss later whether and to what extent Figgis's theory can be said to be inconsistent with the idea of a unitary state. It is, however, true that Gierke was an idealist in philosophy and saw society, in idea, as a moral unity, in a way which Figgis would have found hard to accept.

If there is one thing which united the thinkers whom we are accustomed to call pluralists it is the rejection of the state as a *moral sovereign*. The theory of Hobbes, which was for Figgis 'the meanest of all ethical theories',[20] based an immoral doctrine of omnipotence upon a false view of human nature; so far from being a creation of man's will, the state is in fact natural and necessary to men, and is no artificial creation of their choice. He attacked the idea that the only body which has rights is the state. M. Emile Combes had declared that the only rights there can be are state rights, and that the only authority which is legitimate is that of the republic. Here we have a theory which is essentially that of Hobbes, where there can be no rights against the sovereign who is morally absolute. This theory, stated Figgis, denies the fact of conscience, the institutions of religion and the reality of family life. He quoted an astonishing statement by Mr Justice Darling to the effect that the law of God can be altered by an Act of Parliament, as evidence that this Hobbist way of thinking was widespread in his own day.[21] Moral sovereignty, the idea that any person or body of persons ought to be obeyed whatever he or it commands is, he thought, a dangerous theory. 'Can you,' he demanded,

> take up a liberal paper to-day without finding appeals to that general will, statements about that popular source of all power, defiance of every person or body of persons who dared to throw his puny . . . preferences against the ungovernable right of the people's will and to stem, as they say, the tide of progress and democratic enlightenment with the obsolete pretences of vested interest?[22]

Yet the theory of natural rights was, he thought, misleading and only resulted from the claim of the state to moral supremacy. When this claim to moral sovereignty goes, then the notion of natural and imprescriptible rights, which arose in opposition to it, must go too.

This conception of objective right, of a higher or natural law, is one which Figgis did not accept in some of his early writings, but his increased fears regarding the claims made on behalf of the state convinced him that there must be some objective standard which secured the liberty of individuals and groups. When he published his first book he rejected concepts of natural law as involving a utopian attempt to find absolute principles in politics. It is, he maintained, impossible to discover an immutable basis for politics and to lift it above considerations of mere expediency. But why is it impossible to discover political principles which are universally applicable? This is not the same as a belief that all nations must be reduced to the same uniform level, but it is merely to state that there are certain values which it is the duty of all states to encourage as best they can in the situation in which they find themselves. This notion of objective right forced itself upon him more and more as he thought about political matters. 'it is this notion of a higher law', he wrote in an unpublished paper,

> which is the basis of all constitutionalism and is one of the legacies of the Middle Ages. It provoked and eventually secured the victory of Parliament in the XVIIth century — after, indeed, when the victory was won ... Parl: took over from the other side the doctrine of an omnipotent sovereign and Whigs like Charles Fox were imbued completely with the notion[23] (which among other results lost us America). In the XVIIth century, however, the contest as far as it was political and not religious was directly between those who claimed for law a supreme place — and those who were obsessed with the new conception of an omnipotent sovereignty.[24]

Other pluralists were equally keen to deny moral sovereignty to any determinate body, although G. D. H. Cole differed from the rest by talking in terms of a general will residing in the people. In so far as the state represents the will of the people, the state is, according to Cole, sovereign.[25] With his conception of a court of functional equity, which would represent men in the fullness of their social relations, comes the corollary of an increasing emphasis on sovereignty.

Full sovereignty, however, was thought to lie in the 'complex of organised associations' within society, and he thought that we cannot get more specific without handing it over to a body of which the function is partial rather than general.[26] As the individual can never fully be represented by associations, not even the most representative body will be completely sovereign. If there is no possibility of finding out where the sovereignty lies, is there much point in talking about it? Ernest Barker, too, thought that sovereignty is not indivisible but is 'multiple and multicellular'.[27] Does this solve the problem of sovereignty? Is it not, on the contrary, true to say that as soon as the concept of sovereignty becomes indeterminate and divided, it becomes vacuous? Perhaps Benoist was wisest when he declared,

> As for sovereignty, let us without remorse drop it from our political vocabulary, for time has set about to erase it.[28]

One of the thinkers who most emphasised the conception of objective right in politics and law, which we are opposing to the notion of moral sovereignty, was Léon Duguit. For him, it is the possession of force which distinguishes the state from other groups. There is no obligation to obey the state as such; its commands are obligatory only when they are just, and when the consequences of obeying them will be better than the result of disobedience. Sovereignty is an attribute of will, and will is a faculty of persons, and as the state is not regarded as a person in Duguit's system, the problem of sovereignty evaporates — there is no such thing as sovereignty. 'We no longer believe', he wrote,

> in the dogma of national sovereignty any more than in the dogma of divine right. The rulers are those who actually have the power of compulsion in their hands . . . power is not a right but simply an ability to act.[29]

Harold Laski was considerably interested in and influenced by the thought of Duguit and Figgis in this matter of sovereignty. Barker tells us that it was Figgis, and through Figgis, Maitland and Gierke, who were the chief influences on Laski in his New College days. Laski in effect reversed the famous dictum of Nettleship that 'will not force is the basis of the state'.[30] The thing which characterises the state is its possession of force and this gives it no inherent right to be obeyed in all matters. Pluralism, he insisted, denies ultimately 'the sovereignty of anything save right conduct'.[31] It is a false theory which would suggest that the will of any person or body of persons is unconditionally binding on the consciences of men. This is why Laski valued Newman's remarks on conscience and sovereignty so highly. Laski and the pluralist writers with whom he was associated were more concerned with discovering what ought to be done than with finding out who has the right to make political decisions. The state is characterised, then, by the fact that it is the organ which possesses overwhelming force in society, but the pluralist denied the rightness of force and rejected the idea that 'the pursuit of evil can be made good by the character of the performer'.[32] In later life Laski saw the essence of the pluralist position as including a belief that the state's title to obedience lies in what it wills rather than in the fact of its willing.

What is needed, Laski maintained, was a new theory of natural law or objective right, which however does not lay down any immutable laws to be applied automatically in all circumstances. He thought that an effort to develop the ideas of the medieval schoolmen on this matter was needed in order that a satisfactory theory of the state should be evolved. It was, in his view, the decline of natural law theories which had led to the rise of ideas about the sovereignty of Parliament. Even such an acute theorist as Morris Cohen apparently failed to grasp, or at least refused to accept, this theory of objective right. His belief that there must always be some body in society which draws the line in disputes, would have been acceptable to the pluralists, or at least to Figgis and to the majority of English pluralists; but he went on to say that 'the state cannot give up its reserve *rights* to limit any form of conscience which it *deems* a nuisance'.[33] Surely the state has only the right to limit forms of conscience which *actually are* threats to the security of the nation or to the liberty of others, not any form which *it deems* a nuisance. If by 'rights' Cohen meant simply legal rights, then there would be little to quarrel with but the context implies moral right. Figgis and Laski would have agreed with L. T. Hobhouse when he declared that the essential mistake of some idealist political philosophers — and, Figgis would have added, the Hobbist who regards the state as the 'mortal god' — was that they regarded the state 'as a kind of divine institution'.[34]

III

The conception of *political sovereignty*, as we have defined it, was also rejected by Figgis. He thought that any talk of a person or body of persons possessing supreme power which will on all occasions triumph is false, misleading and perhaps dangerous. In addition to rejecting the moral theory of sovereignty, as a political philosophy, he refused to accept the popular idea that there is or must be in every state a body which is politically supreme. It is not the case that in any dispute the state, in Britain, would be sure to prevail; it is possible that a church or important trade union could fight successfully against a decree of the state. Whether there are rights against the state or not, as Figgis pointed out, people think that there are; there is always the possibility of civil war, and it is a false social theory which ignores this fact. There is no single identifiable body in Britain which can get its way whatever it commands. Does it solve the problem by saying that 'the people' or 'public opinion' are sovereign? We have seen that it can hardly be said to do so.

Laski also attacked the concept of political sovereignty, which insists that there must be in every social order some single centre of ultimate reference, some power that is able to resolve disputes by saying a last word that will be obeyed.[35] He regarded society as a parallelogram of forces in which different elements prevailed on different occasions. Ernest Barker also found the conception of political sovereignty unacceptable: on one occasion this society would prevail, on another that; and there is no body which can be relied upon to win in all circumstances. MacIver believed that the opposition of large groups to government policy can in many instances prevent the carrying out of that policy. A. D.

Lindsay also asserted that the state has control over the activities of groups and individuals only in so far as the citizens are prepared to give it this power; and this willingness is always limited:

> Wherever, therefore, men's loyalty to a non-political association, a class, or a church, or a trade union is greater than their loyalty to the State, the State's power over the trade unions or churches or classes within it is thereby diminished.[36]

G. D. H. Cole, however, differed from other pluralists in this matter. He wrote of the sovereignty of the whole community, and believed that this sovereignty could be represented — though imperfectly — by a federal body, including the state (as the association of consumers) and other functional associations. He even wrote of an 'ultimate body' which everyone but anarchists must believe to be sovereign.[37]

IV

The problem of *legal sovereignty* is a complicated one. Figgis never appears to have wished to challenge the doctrine that, for the purposes of lawyers, the enactments of the British Parliament are not to be questioned. In an earlier period he was quite prepared to accept the idea of the supremacy of Parliament as a legal theory, as well as a practical guide to lawyers. He declared that Coke, with a common law theorists,

> had not really grasped the conception of sovereignty; he maintained a position, reasonable enough in the Middle Ages, but impossible in a developed unitary State.[38]

He believed that Locke was guilty of a confusion between natural law and positive law, and praised theorists of the divine right of kings for a deeper insight into the nature of law than their opponents, who were 'ever haunted by the vain illusion of placing legal limits on the sovereign power'.[39] The Jesuit and whig theories which taught that law which is not just is not really law, and ought not to be obeyed, were thought by him to be of little value, and the idea that contracts could be binding apart from the positive commands of the sovereign 'seems nonsense to us, as Austin showed'.[40]

As time progressed he began, chiefly under the influence of Maitland, to doubt the value of the Austinian theory. Even at the time of his first book he confessed that it would be difficult to fit the feudal system of law and society into Austin's idea of sovereignty. Gradually he came to doubt the whole of Austin's theory. If we take it as it stands, when the sovereign is one — political and legal — it is, as various thinkers have pointed out, difficult to accept; but when all the substance has been taken out of the theory and political sovereignty has evaporated into indeterminancy, the conception is theoretically useless. If in fact the legal sovereign is politically responsible and cannot do what it likes (in Austin's theory it was not responsible in this sense, as the legal and political sovereigns were one) then as a theory of law it is valueless. A legal theory which does not apply to the world as we know it is not a particularly useful one. 'It is,' Figgis declared of the Austinian theory,

> either fallacious or so profoundly inadequate as to have no more than a verbal justification. One begins by thinking Austin self-evident, one learns that many qualifications have to be made, and finally one ends by treating his whole method as abstract and theoretic.[41]

If the theory of legal sovereignty simply means that judges in Britain ought not to question an Act of Parliament, then there can be little objection to it,[42] but if it means that a law is merely the command of Parliament it is either false or inadequate. We have to introduce qualifications such as 'what it permits it commands' and that the state itself only submits to the process of law by the courtesy of auto-limitation. In fact it is not a question of Parliament's deciding to permit certain things, but of its not being able to do anything else. As Duguit saw, the whole modern conception of the administrative state demands that the state be responsible in the law courts for its actions; many of the acts of the state are not commands, and they operate in spheres in which the state is not able to command.

Laski was, on the whole, in agreement with Figgis on this question; 'Legally', he stated,

no one can deny that there exists in every state some organ
whose authority is unlimited. But that legality is no more
than a fiction of logic.[43]

Yet, as we have seen, even this is doubtful. He thought that
the theory which speaks of law in these terms is of purely
formal interest and is likely to lead the unwary into dangerous waters. Legal absolutism, he thought, passes easily
into political absolutism, as the term 'right' can be, and is,
used in both contexts. Lawyers, however, are loathe to abandon the idea of legal sovereignty, as they find it useful in
practice.[44] Holmes thought that 'from a (sound) legal point
of view'[45] the ideas of Figgis and Laski were false. Holmes
and Pollock spilt much ink lamenting the influence of Figgis
on the young Laski. 'It was', thought Pollock, 'an ill day for
him when he fell into the hands of Figgis.'[46]

Perhaps the theory of legal sovereignty has been useful in
one aspect; the recognition by judges of the supremacy of
Parliament in legal matters has preserved England from what
a schoolboy claimed to be the American tradition: 'A government not of men but of lawyers'. In practice the idea might
be useful, but could we not say equally well, as Gierke did,
that the state is the authority in modern society which has
the duty of formulating laws, and that the law courts must
recognise this? But law, Gierke argued, is not the creation of
a sovereign state, it is merely formulated and rationalised by
the state in modern societies. Both law and the state emanate
from the life of the community; the state is not the offspring
of law (as in the natural law theories) any more than the law
is the child of the state (as in the Austinian conception).
Duguit, however, put law above the state, and found this view
of Gierke's untenable. 'It attempts on the one hand', he said,

> to reconcile the autonomy of the individual with the
> omnipotence of the State and, on the other hand, to
> subordinate the State to law, while maintaining that it is
> omnipotent.[47]

It is certainly difficult to see how Gierke's theory would
work out in practice; he would probably have said that in so
far as the state is a true state it will enact true law.

The state is not even in law free to command just what it likes. There are occasions on which the state is forced to accept certain facts and to recognise them legally (such as in the case of the personality of groups which will be discussed in a later chapter). It may be agreed that so far as the state attempts to force upon the law courts a system which is unworkable, as the non-recognition of group personality would be, it is not merely making bad law, but is not making law at all. It is essential to the concept of law that it be applied (imperfectly perhaps, and with interpretation) in the law courts, and in so far as the state ignores social facts and forces an unworkable system upon the courts it is to that extent not making law. If the system of statutes were to become so out of touch with social reality as we know it, were ignored by the people, and were incapable of enforcement by the courts, would it fall under our conception of law at all? It is at least plausible to doubt it. If it is in fact impossible to divorce law from society and from politics, then a concept of legal sovereignty and a command theory of law are liable to lead to a political theory which denies the rights of individuals and groups. It is not merely a confusion of language that is responsible for ideas of legal, political and moral sovereignty being called by the same name. Unless legal theory is to be divorced from social and moral theory, a concept of legal sovereignty will lead a man to talk and think in terms of moral and political sovereignty. This fact may be illustrated by the language of a fairly liberal Austinian:

> The state's will is sovereign, and therefore subject to no regulation from above; its powers over members are numerous, indefinite, and irresistible; and its purposes, general rather than special, touch human life at every point.[48]

It was the political and moral implications of the concept of legal sovereignty which led Figgis and the pluralists to attack it. If we were to adopt the Austinian criterion of law, we would have to deny that international law is truly law; many legal theorists have been led on from this to deny any role to a judicial or quasi judicial system of international control. This is one of the reasons why Figgis thought that the Austinian theory was dangerous; it amounts to what some philosophers would call a persuasive definition.

I shall sum up Figgis's conception of law by quoting a fairly long passage from an unpublished lecture:

> One school represented by John Austin fixes upon the coercive element in all positive law and . . . makes of law above all things a command — and grounds it in some way or other on force. The other school looks at the objects of law, its universality, its aim, its connection with the State . . . and fixes its thought on its content. It sees in law the sacrament of justice, the symbol of something beyond and above human affairs, an attempt of a human society to conform to the eternal principle of right. This school is represented by what Austin had the impertinence to call the 'fustian description' of law in Hooker. . . . The other is expressed in the famous lectures of Austin on Jurisprudence and gives the definition of law as a command set by a person or persons politically sovereign to a person or persons politically subject.
>
> Even Austin had to go beyond a mere command — for he includes the conception of generality, and will not admit a mere particular command to be a law, probably not a tax. Austin's definition was practically the notion of law which came from the Renaissance lawyers and political philosophers — represented by men such as Bodin and Hobbes — and has reference to a fully developed compact State with an irresistible government. No one can deny that it has in it elements of truth — or that it describes one aspect of law — but it is not all. It lays too much stress on one element, that of command with its corollary force. It has in practice a very evil political reaction — for it tends to foster the notion, that not merely legally but morally the sovereign may do whatever he pleases.
>
> Both doctrines can be traced back to the Roman jurisprudence — the latter [i.e. the command theory] to the idea of imperial power — to the maxims *quod principi placuit, legibus solutus* and so forth. The former to the notion of law as *ars aequi et boni*, to the conception of equity and the dictates of natural law, which may explain and if need be override the positive.[49]

Thus Figgis and the pluralists were dissatisfied with the theory, or rather theories, of sovereignty which had support in their day. So far as the moral, political and legal sovereigns were united in one person or body (as in Hobbes) the theory was immoral; so far as the political and legal sovereigns were united (as in Austin) the theory was untrue to the facts, unless made tautological; and any theory which separated all three tended to be so empty that — apart from the assertion that the law courts in Britain cannot go behind the Acts of Parliament — it was misleading and even dangerous. Once the idea that will is the basis of obligation be rejected the theory of sovereignty will collapse.

The rejection of state sovereignty was an essential preliminary to the formation of a political philosophy of pluralism. If the state is morally sovereign, then groups and individuals can never have rights against the state. A notion of political sovereignty will undermine the sociological idea of group personality, and the whole possibility of a plural society is called into question by state omnipotence. A narrow construction of legal sovereignty removes from the sphere of law the system of common law which is the basis of most of the guarantees of group life, while construed widely the statement of the theory is analytic, though still perhaps misleading. It is thus clear that a demolition of the notion of state sovereignty was a necessary preliminary to the setting forth of a theory of political pluralism.

4 Group Personality

Political pluralism, as set forth by the group of thinkers we are considering in this essay, is essentially bound up with the idea of group personality. It is convenient to discuss this idea first in its sociological, and then in its legal aspects. The order is important for, as we shall see, those theorists who spoke of the real personality of groups in law insisted that their legal ideas were rooted in social facts.

By the end of the nineteenth century the individualism associated with such writers as Bentham and J. S. Mill was being violently attacked from many quarters. Philosophers, sociologists and social psychologists joined forces to discredit individualism. Perhaps the most telling criticisms came from the sociologists, whose very discipline depends upon the denial of at least some forms of individualism. Herbert Spencer appears to mark the turning point, for he combined a sturdy and, at times, quite fanatical individualism with a belief in 'society' as an organism, which has grown and developed in the same way that a biological organism develops. Society, for Spencer, is not to be seen as a collection of individuals, but as an organism of which the 'large divisions' are families, trade organisations and other groups. Society becomes more and more complex as it develops and as the interdependence of the parts increases. Sir Henry Maine also wrote of a society as an organism, and pointed out that human society did not originate in a series of contracts between isolated individuals, but began as a closed hierarchical structure based upon status. In early societies a man's position is determined by his place in the complex of traditional groups into which he has been born, and history shows men gradually emancipating themselves from this closed society, and placing themselves in associations and in relationships of their own choice. Maine regarded groups as of primary importance, being the cells out of which the body politic is formed.[1]

Curiously, neither Spencer nor Maine carried the conclusions of his social theories into his political theory. Both *The Man vs the State* and *Popular Government* fail to take seriously the organic nature of human associations and the importance of groups in the state. They are individualistic to the point of absurdity.[2]

Among sociologists, Emile Durkheim played a vital role in the increasing recognition of group life. It is through his membership of groups that the individual develops his personality, according to the French sociologist. Perhaps Durkheim went too far in this attempt to explain all social phenomena in terms of the group, playing down the importance of individual psychology. This is particularly evident in his study on suicide. Durkheim insisted that the group is an entity distinct from its members, with a will of its own. The group thinks and behaves quite differently from the way in which its members would if they were isolated. It must, therefore, he insisted, be treated as an entity *sui generis*. Durkheim claimed to have come to this conclusion not by means of idealist metaphysics but as a result of his attempt to pursue the study of societies in a scientific and empirical manner. Durkheim is particularly significant from our point of view because he saw the political implications of his social theories. In a penetrating criticism of collectivism he pointed out that merely for the state to take over the means of production would solve none of the deeper problems of society:

> Where the state is the only environment in which men can live communal lives they inevitably lose contact, become detached, and thus society disintegrates. A nation can be maintained only if, between the State and the individual, there is intercalated a whole series of secondary groups near enough to the individuals to attract them strongly in their sphere of action and drag them, in this way, into the general torrent of social life.[3]

Durkheim can certainly be regarded as one of the precursors of syndicalism in France, though he would by no means have accepted the more extreme varieties of this theory.

In England sociologists like L. T. Hobhouse, and social psychologists like W. McDougall agreed with the basic methodological conclusion of Durkheim that groups must be studied as entities in themselves and not broken down into their component individual members.

The revival of philosophical idealism in the last half of the nineteenth century in Britain, associated with the names of F. H. Bradley, B. Bosanquet, T. H. Green and the Caird brothers, also contributed to the decline in individualism. In his *Ethical Studies* (1876) Bradley assailed the idea that society is nothing but an artificial collection of isolated individuals, and that these individuals are the only 'real' entities. The individual is what he is because of his membership of groups which have an existence just as real as that of individual persons. He went on to point out that

> there are such facts as the family, then in a middle position a man's own profession and society, and, over all, the larger community of the state. . . . That objective institutions exist is of course an obvious fact; and it is a fact which every day is becoming plainer that these institutions are organic, and further, that they are moral.[4]

Green also pointed to the importance of group life, and spoke of the state as 'a society of societies', a phrase later to be used by some of the pluralists.

Those writers with whom we are principally concerned agreed with the sociologists in their criticism of 'methodological individualism', as Karl Popper would call it, and insisted that groups must be studied as entities in themselves. Further, they went on to argue that personal categories may properly be applied to them. Perhaps it was Otto von Gierke, interpreted and presented to the English reader by F. W. Maitland, who most influenced the pluralist writers in their notions of group personality. Gierke was essentially a legal theorist, and his ideas will be examined in greater detail in a later section of this chapter. His legal theories, as we shall see, were based upon sociological conclusions about the nature of group life. Maitland reminded his readers that we speak of

the will of the nation, the mind of the legislature, the
settled policy of one State, the ambitious designs of
another.[5]

The best proof for Maitland that the realists mean business is
that they take their groups into the law courts and markets
and make them stand up to the wear and tear of business and
legal life. Group personality was for Maitland no mere legal
fiction. The 'morality of common sense' recognises the group
as a moral entity.

Following Maitland and Gierke, Figgis too insisted on the
real personality of groups. 'What do we find as a fact?' he
demanded:

> Not, surely, a sand-heap of individuals, all equal and un-
> differentiated, unrelated except to the State, but an ascen-
> ding hierarchy of groups, family, school, town, county,
> union, Church, etc., etc. . . . In the real world, the isolated
> individual does not exist; he begins always as a member of
> something, and, as I said earlier, his personality can
> develop only in society.[6]

Figgis laid special emphasis upon the 'small associations
which mould the life of men more intimately than does the
great collectivity we call the State'.[7] But at the same time he
warned against any tendency so to submerge the individual in
the group that he loses his distinct personality. In one of his
last books, *The Will to Freedom*, he saw this danger more
clearly than in his earlier works. The group is an entity just as
real as its individual members, and has an 'inherent life', not
depending upon the state, and thus has the power of developing and growing. Figgis's insistence upon the right of a
group to develop, and change its purpose, has important legal
implications which I shall consider in a later section. Although he was himself particularly concerned with religious
groups, he insisted that his theory applies to all groups, and
that it does not make a special case of the church. In fact, he
claimed that his social theory should be acceptable to liberal-
minded secularists for this very reason: it does not demand
special treatment for religious groups. In this, Figgis differed
from a writer like P. T. Forsyth who, although claiming to

derive his ideas partly from Figgis, made a special case of the church, the personality of which is 'a gift and moral prerogative from God'. A religious group is not, he went on to say, 'a member of the State in any such sense as a municipality is'.[8] Figgis, on the other hand, believed that, sociologically, religious groups must be regarded in basically the same way as secular groups. As will be made clear in a later chapter, Figgis did not conceive of the state as another group in society alongside trade unions, churches and commercial enterprises. He did not think of the state as possessing a personality.

Harold Laski insisted that a group possesses personality in the sense of being 'a binding together of its individual parts to certain modes of behaviour deemed by them likely to promote the interests with which they are concerned'.[9] Societies, he wrote, are persons just as individuals are persons, having a character, ethos and identity of their own; they therefore are morally responsible for their actions.[10] As we shall see, some critics of the pluralists attack them for not recognising that the state has a right to claim personality just as much as any other group in the community. As we have noted, Figgis did not think of the state in these terms; the state is a collection of groups. Laski, however, maintained that states, as well as other associations, can be spoken of as persons. 'The reality of the State's personality', Laski insisted, 'is a compulsion we may not resist'.[11] Many writers, however, did resist the compulsion and, later, Laski himself joined them. He gradually came to reject this 'realist' conception of group personality, partly after having considered the powerful arguments of Morris Cohen, in his article on 'Communal Ghosts'. In his *Grammar of Politics* an earlier realism was modified; later it was completely rejected. In 1948 Laski wrote: 'A group of human beings is not a person, in the sense that each member of the group is a person . . . the corporate "person", in short, is not a person over and above its members.'[12] Yet even in his earlier writings he interpreted the concept of a 'group will' or a 'group mind' in an individualist sense. The group mind is the mind 'of a number of men who, actuated by some common purpose, are capable of a unified activity'.[13]

G. D. H. Cole also moved away from his early insistence on

group personality. In 1914 he claimed that social science and social philosophy are basically concerned with 'the phenomenon of collective personality', and was even prepared to use the term 'group soul'.[14] Later, however, Cole came to reject the idea of group personality; personality belongs only to the individual man or woman. In his essay on *Social Theory* (1920) he insisted that the only kind of personality which a group possesses is legal personality, and that here the concept is a purely technical one. Nevertheless he claimed that the analogy of a person is nearer to the truth than the mechanical or organic analogies, though to ascribe personality to a group is likely to lead to confusion and to obscure the difference between individual and associative actions.

Thus we see in Laski and Cole a gradual move away from the notion of group personality. A suspicion of the concept was earlier voiced by Ernest Barker. He was himself considerably influenced by the ideas of Maitland and Figgis, but warned that 'to talk of the real personality of anything, other than the individual human being, is to indulge in dubious and perhaps nebulous speech'.[15] Barker suggested that the pluralism in society is not ultimately constituted by a plurality of groups but by sets of *ideas*. The struggle is between competing 'schemes in which real and individual persons and wills are related to one another by means of a common and organizing idea'.[16] Figgis and the other early pluralists could hardly have accepted this theory of Barker. Trade unions, clubs, families and churches are tied together by links much more powerful than 'organizing ideas'. The struggle between Bismarck's Germany and the Roman Catholic Church, known as the *Kulturkampf*, was not a struggle between two sets of organising ideas, but between two very concrete groups, each claiming the loyalty of its members (many of whom belonged to both groups). Much of the anti-clericalism in France in the early part of the present century was not so much the result of a dislike of religious *ideas*, as an objection to the very concrete claims which a religious group was making on the loyalty of its members. It was these groups to which people like Emile Combes objected, owing to the challenge which they were thought to present to the state. Many men have died for family or friends, for church or for nation, but who would be willing to die for an 'organizing idea'? Barker's position is surely less tenable than that of the other pluralists on this matter of group personality.

The idea of group personality, or the belief that group life is 'real', was then central to the ideas of the English political pluralists; when Laski and Cole moved away from a belief in group personality they moved away from pluralism. The controversies between the pluralists and their adversaries about the nature of group life continues in our own day. There are those still who believe that the way to understand the life of a group is to understand the individual components and to see how they interact. This individualist approach is adopted by H. Simon and C. I. Barnard in organisation theory; in fields of social and political philosophy one could mention Karl Popper, F. A. Hayek and Isaiah Berlin. John Wisdom put the position as follows: 'to say anything about a nation is merely to say something (though not the same thing) about its nationals.'[17] Susan Stebbing has told us that we can talk about 'Germany', 'Great Britain' or 'Italy' if we like, so long as we recognise that these are only 'abstractions', and that it is dangerous to 'take these names for single entities'.[18] Although this group of writers would claim to be 'empiricist', we look in vain for empirical support for these assertions. If it is true that to say anything about a group is merely to say something about its individual members, is it also true that to say something about individual men is to say something about their limbs, and that to say something about their limbs is simply to say something about their cells? Surely we may say that groups are as 'real' as individuals. The physicist would see men as composed of atoms or electric charges, which for him are the 'real' units; the biologists talks in terms of organs which are 'real' for him. For the preacher or the moralist the individual is the basic unit; the social worker might think in terms of families or other social groups. None of these entities is any more real than the other.

Most social and organisation theorists today recognise the validity of the group as an entity *sui generis*, and are opposed to the reductionism of the individualists. Writers like Elton Mayo, Kurt Lewin, E. W. Bakke, G. Homans and P. Selznick reject reductionism. Selznick puts his own position as follows:

> Day-to-day decisions, relevant to the actual problems met in the translation of policy into action, create precedents, alliances, effective symbols, and personal loyalties which transform the organisation from a profane, manipulable instrument into something having a sacred status and thus resistant to treatment simply as a means to some external goal.[19]

This methodological realism with respect to groups has certain important political and legal implications. Politically, we recognise that the group has an existence which is not derived from the state, just as the life of individuals is not thus derived; legally, we conclude that it should be treated as a 'person' in law, with duties and responsibilities which cannot be resolved into the duties and responsibilities of individual members of the group, with a developing life of its own, and with the possibility that the group may acquire new objects, thus modifying its original purpose.

The ideas of group personality which were advocated by the political pluralist had important legal implications. They rejected the 'fiction' theory of legal personality, and the 'concession' theory which usually goes with it, and suggested alternative positions. I shall first deal with the fiction theory and its consequences, and then look at the alternative 'realist' theory as put forward by Otto von Gierke and his followers. The pluralist writers with whom this monograph is particularly concerned were not primarily legal theorists, but we shall see the way in which they took sides on these issues of group personality, owing to the social and political consequences which follow from the legal disputes. The legal arguments on the question of group personality have been extremely complicated, and at times confused. Considering the problem of corporate personality, Dicey wrote in 1904: 'If, then, the law be confused, it all the more accurately reflects the spirit of the time.'[20]

The fiction theory was formulated by Savigny, who declared it to have been the theory which was orthodox in

Roman law. According to this theory the only jurally capable person is the individual man; only he can, under the perfect system, be the subject of rights. He is the only real entity recognised by the law. Yet some modifications need to be made in this theory for the sake of convenience. 'Nevertheless,' he wrote,

> this original idea of a person may undergo a twofold modification by Positive Law . . . by being restricted or expanded. A Jural Capacity may, for instance, in the first place, be either wholly or partially denied to many individual Men; it may, in the second place, be transferred to something external to the individual Man, and thus a Juristical Person may by this means be artificially created.[21]

The fiction theory thus assumes that the individual man is in some way a real person in law, while the group is a fictitious person. Gierke traced the theory back as far as Innocent IV, though this has led to some controversy.[22] There is some evidence that the fiction theory was assumed by many English lawyers before being set forth by Savigny. Thus in the famous *Sutton's Hospital* Case[23] Coke stated that corporate personality 'rests only in intendment and consideration of the law', while Blackstone referred to groups as artificial persons. Sir Frederick Pollock, however, in an essay presented to Gierke on his eightieth birthday, argued skilfully that the English common law has never accepted a clear theory of legal personality. He pointed out that the word 'artificial' does not necessarily mean 'fictitious', but merely 'in accordance with the rules of art'.[24] The fiction theory, as set forth by Savigny, gained considerable popularity in the nineteenth century, however, and usually carried with it the corollary that if groups were only fictitious then they must be given their personality by some body, and this body is the state. Groups receive their personality as a concession from the state.

Otto von Gierke began in earnest the assault upon the fiction theory and the concession theory of group personality.[25] Gierke denied that all law originates with the state; the state has no logical priority over the law — they are interdependent. He therefore looked critically at the concession theory of group personality. Gierke's sociological presuppositions were sympathetic to the idea of the real personality of a group. He argued that a group has a real existence which is more than the sum of its parts, and believed that groups possess many of the same characteristics as individual men. 'We find above the level of individual existence', he declared,

> a second, independent level of existence of human collective associations. Above the individual spirit, the individual will, the individual consciousness, we recognise in thousandfold expression of life the real existence of common spirit, common will, and common consciousness.[26]

He maintained that sociological investigation only confirms what we know by common sense: that we do not live as isolated individuals, but that we find our fullest development in a vast number of associations and groups, culminating in the state. If the life of groups is a sociological phenomenon, Gierke argued, then the law should recognise this fact. 'Is it not, however, possible', he demanded,

> that law, when it treats organised associations as persons, is not disregarding reality, but giving reality more adequate expression? Is it not possible that human associations are real unities which receive through legal recognition of their personality only what corresponds to their real nature? I, with many others, answer, Yes.[27]

We have here, then, a legal theory which is closely connected to a sociological theory, and when it burst upon England in 1900 with Maitland's translation of part of *Das deutsche Genossenschaftsrecht* its assumptions were not always very well understood. Gierke's ideas, however, seem to have had a double effect in England. In the first place the purely legal conception of the personality of groups was changing, and the fiction theory in its old formulation was being found increasingly unsatisfactory. Judges more and more found themselves treating groups as they treated individual persons, and legal theorists were searching for a more adequate explanation of legal practice than was furnished by the fiction theory. Gierke's theory helped to supply this need. Secondly,

Gierke's ideas, as interpreted by Maitland, provided material for the development of political pluralism.

By the beginning of the twentieth century there was considerable dissatisfaction with the fiction theory of group personality. Coke's dictum that 'none but the king alone can create or make a corporation'[28] was, strictly speaking, untrue even in his own day. There are and have been recognised for many centuries corporations in common law and corporations by implication. Also, by the first decade of the twentieth century, it was clear that the rigid distinction which many people had maintained between corporate and unincorporated bodies was breaking down. In the *Taff Vale* case a trade union, though not an incorporated body, was treated for legal purposes as a person and was sued by employers for damages incurred during a strike which had been organised by the union. Trade unions, declared Lord Atkinson, in a later and equally celebrated case,

> are, when registered, quasi-corporations, resembling much more closely railway companies incorporated by statute than voluntary associations of individuals merely bound together by contract or agreement, express or implied.[29]

By 1924 Sir Paul Vinogradoff was able to declare that there is no clear distinction between corporations and other permanent groups and that they shade off into one another. Thus, construed narrowly, the statement that legal personality is a gift of the state is patently false. Construed broadly, it is true, necessarily true. If we include in 'the state' the common law and the activities of the law courts — if we say that legal personality is bestowed upon groups and upon individuals by legal practice — then we are right, by definition, for that is what legal personality means.

Legal theory is based upon legal practice, and it is worth looking at the way in which groups are treated in English and American law. It was generally agreed, and the House of Lords confirmed quite clearly in a celebrated case, *Salomon v. Salomon*, that a corporation is a person distinct from the individual persons who compose it. But it was generally held that corporations, unlike individual persons, could not commit torts which demand a guilty intention, nor crimes which

require *mens rea*. In 1854 Lord Alderson held that an action
for malicious prosecution cannot be brought against a company, because a corporate person does not have a will and is
therefore incapable of malice (*Stevens* case). Later, in the
same century, Lord Bramwell declared: 'I am at a loss to
understand how there could be corporate malice' (*Henderson*
case). Nevertheless with the increased numbers of corporations and quasi corporations, and with the obvious injustices
that individuals suffered at their hands, some modification in
legal practice was demanded. In a series of cases in the 1880s
and 1890s the civil law was modified on this matter (*Edwards*
case, *Kent* case, *Cornford* case, *Barwick* case). 'It is obvious',
declared Fry in the first of these cases,

> that great evils would arise if, on the ground that a
> corporation can have no mind, and therefore can have no
> malice, a corporation were able to escape from that
> liability which if they [sic] were not incorporated they
> would have to bear.

Thus by the end of the nineteenth century legal practice in
civil law had moved away from some of the worst consequences of the fiction theory.

It was also held by many fictitionists that corporations
cannot be guilty of criminal offences which demand a *mens
rea*. In *R. v. Cory Bros.* the court found that a railway
company was not guilty of a criminal offence if it erected an
electric fence against which an employee fell and was killed; a
company cannot have a *mens rea*. Nevertheless, things have
changed; in a later case, *I. C. R. Haulage*, Justice Stable
commented on the decision in *Cory:*

> If the matter came before the court today, the result might
> well be different. . . . this is a branch of the law to which
> the attitude of the courts has in the passage of time
> undergone a process of development.

So another plank in the fiction theory gave way. In the same
year (1944) Lord Caldecote said:

> the real point which we have to decide . . . is . . . whether a
> company is capable of an act of will or a state of mind, so

as to be able to form an intention to deceive or to have knowledge of the truth or falsity of a statement.[30]

Legal practice can therefore be said to have moved away from the dogmas of the fiction theory, which as Maitland saw in 1900 had received notice to quit. The theory was practically unworkable as well as being logically untenable.

One question which particularly concerned Figgis was whether the law should recognise the right of a group to develop and change its purpose. If the group is sociologically a real entity, with a life of its own, then surely it will grow and develop. If the law is going to recognise this fact of the real personality of groups, then the law must, according to him, recognise the right of groups to develop and to determine for themselves the limits of this development. It was the *Free Church of Scotland* case which brought this issue to a head for Figgis. In 1843 the Scottish Church had split; almost a third of the Church, led by Thomas Chalmers and others, severed its connection with the state to form the Free Church of Scotland. The Disruption, as it was called, was mainly caused by demands for a change in the patronage system, so that more power in the selection of ministers would be given to the local congregation. The Free Church believed in the establishment principle, and was Calvinist in theology. In 1900, after many years of discussion, the Free Church, under Principal Rainy, combined with the United Presbyterian Church, which had been formed in 1847 by a union of the United Secession Church and the Relief Synod. The United Presbyterians were somewhat more liberal in their interpretation of Calvinism than were the founders of the Free Church; nor did they accept the principle of church establishment. The union was approved by 643 votes to 27 in the Assembly of the Free Church, but the dissidents (popularly known as the Wee Frees) took the case to court claiming that the action of the majority was *ultra vires*, and that they were themselves the true successors of the Free Church. The case eventually reached the House of Lords which, after wallowing in questions as unfamiliar to them as the development of doctrine and the meaning of the Westminster Confession, decided that the action of the majority had contravened the original trust and that all the property of the church must go to the Wee Frees. The main point at issue was whether the two principles — establishment and the Westminster Confession's interpretation of Calvinism — were fundamental in the original trust, and in the minds of the founders of the Free Church. The church itself, through its constituted machinery had declared by an overwhelming majority that they were not fundamental; but the Lords decided otherwise. The Free Church (i.e. the majority who wished for union) argued that any person joining the church thereby submitted to its organ of authority, and that this authority had decided that these matters were not fundamental to the church.

As Figgis saw, certain important issues were at stake here. Were the courts incapable of conceiving the development of purpose within a living body? Was it right for the courts to go behind the constituted authority of the church in deciding what is fundamental to that body? How strict should the courts be in their application of the doctrine of *ultra vires* and of the binding nature of trust deeds? These were some of the questions raised in the case and discussed by Figgis in *Churches in the Modern State*.

The doctrine of *ultra vires* in corporation law is a difficult one to apply. If a body which was founded to provide old ladies with radios suddenly decided to spend its money on Rolls Royce cars for its staff, the courts would declare that this was illegal. A railway company cannot (or could not) apply its funds to purposes other than those specified in the act of incorporation, 'If the great body of shareholders', said Kindersley V. C.,

> agree to carry on a business different from that for which the company was constituted, a single shareholder has a right to say that it shall not be done, and may apply for and obtain an injunction.[31]

In the case of unincorporated bodies the trust deeds form a similar limit.

With regard to *ultra vires* in company law, the Cohen Committee reported in 1945 that

> we think that every company, whether incorporated before or after the passing of a new Companies Act, should,

notwithstanding anything omitted from its memorandum of association, have as regards third parties the same power as an individual.[32]

This clear-cut solution, of eliminating the whole concept of *ultra vires* in this context was not, however, accepted. Section 5 of the Companies Act 1948 greatly extended the power of companies to alter their memoranda, though as one authority on the subject has remarked, 'the *ultra vires* doctrine seems to have outlived its usefulness'.[33] But the case of a church is somewhat different from that of a company, and if the law on this question has liberalised with regard to the memoranda of the latter, it should have liberalised all the more with regard to the trust deeds of churches. Is it not possible to treat a religious body more like an individual with powers of development, rather than like a dead thing, tied to the exact formulation of a document, as was done in the *Free Church* case? It was, as Maitland observed, an unfortunate day when this case was decided and the 'dead hand fell with a resounding slap upon the living body'.[34]

Figgis was thus demanding that the doctrine of *ultra vires* and the interpretation of trust deeds should be applied in a much more elastic way, and that the courts should be more willing to recognise the facts of group life than they had up to his time. He recognised that his position in this matter was consistent with theological notions of the development of Christian doctrine, similar to those set forth by J. H. Newman. 'Belief in the Catholic Church', wrote Figgis, 'is belief in development; and this means a creative evolution'.[35] The courts should normally be prepared to accept the decisions of the constituted authority within a group about the kind of developments which are desirable. This position agrees in substance with that which was later maintained by the Cohen Committee with respect to company law.

A recent case in the United States brought out the issue once more. In the *Kedroff* case there was a dispute between the majority of the Russian Orthodox Christians in the U.S.A. who had severed communion with the Moscow patriarchate, and the body which was still in communion with Moscow, regarding the possession of St Nicholas Cathedral in New York. A law was passed in New York State which had the effect of giving the cathedral to the dissident body. The Supreme Court found this statute to be contrary to the Fourteenth Amendment, and decided that the cathedral should be returned to the body which was in communion with Moscow. This was in many ways a more difficult case than the *Free Church of Scotland* case. Although the majority of church members were in the dissident body, the Russian church is not ruled by majority government. The constituted authority was not an elected body. Justices Reed and Frankfurter insisted that the court does not have a right to impose upon a religious society a form of majority government. As one writer commented:

> Figgis and Maitland would surely have applauded the opinion of Mr Justice Reed in the *Kedroff* case, for it seems to apply the principle of pluralism to the relationships of Church and State in just such a way as they had urged.[36]

Figgis does not, however, make it clear what his position would be if the constituted authority of the religious body decided on one course of action and the 'real life' of the group continued along another course. Should the courts never look behind the constituted authority? In his discussion of the *Free Church* case, Figgis spoke of the rights of the 'overwhelming majority'. In this particular case the two coincided, but they need not always do so. Discussing whether the changes of the English reformation were legally valid in the sense of being 'the work of the hierarchy, and conformed to the legal traditions of the church', he declared,

> Suppose they did not, which seems to me much more probable, irregularities of procedure do not of themselves determine the life of a society. It is not easy to destroy a living society.[37]

Here, he would seem to be arguing that it might be right to look behind the constitutional façade at the real life of the group.

As might be expected, Figgis welcomed the *Taff Vale* decision which treated trade unions as legal persons, in spite of the fact that they were unincorporated. The fact that the Trades Disputes Act of 1906 declared them immune for certain purposes did not destroy the force of the decision. L. C. Webb wrote of 'Figgis's failure to see that the *Taff Vale* decision, which he welcomed enthusiastically, . . . was bitterly resented by the whole trade union movement and was ultimately reversed by legislation'.[38] If Mr Webb had read *Churches in the Modern State* more carefully, he would have seen that Figgis was fully aware of both these things. The decision, he wrote, 'showed that Trades Unions were personalities, in spite of their own wishes'.[39]

It is true to say, then, that by the period of the First World War the fiction theory of group personality had been thoroughly discredited. 'We have heard', remarked Pollock,

> certainly that fictions may pass for facts on the strength of their antiquity, but it would be rather novel to say that facts, when they have existed long enough, become legal fictions, abstractions, *entia rationis*.[40]

Maitland, Figgis and Laski attacked the idea that group personality in law is a mere fiction; they insisted that behind the legal person lay a real entity, and that the law must recognise reality if it is to be an effective instrument of social control. They denied that this legal personality was arbitrarily conferred by the state (i.e. the government). Yet in their more clear-sighted moments they saw that *all* legal personality (including that of the individual) is 'artificial', and that it is created by being recognised in legal practice. Laski wrote that the group has 'an interest to promote, a function to serve. The State does not call it into being. It is not, *outside the categories of law*, dependent upon the State'.[41] In his earlier years Laski was torn between the realism of Gierke and Maitland who believed that groups including the state were real persons, and the positivism of Duguit who rejected the whole idea of real personality.

Many criticisms have been directed against the political pluralists' idea of group personality. It is sometimes suggested that the whole controversy was simply about words, and that there was no substantial issue at stake between the realists and the fictionists. I have already noted that there is some ambiguity in saying that legal personality is the concession of the state; nevertheless, there were significant differences between the realists and their adversaries, and the patronising attitude of Glanville Williams is quite unjustified:

> A vast and fruitless controversy has raged over the question whether corporations aggregate are 'real' or 'fictitious' persons. ... It is submitted that the question is a spurious one and that there is no issue of fact between the two sides. The 'realists' say that an association of men is 'real', but this the 'fictitionists' do not deny. The 'realists' say further that an association of men is itself a 'person'; but this is simply an assertion of the determination of these writers to use the word 'person' in a certain way, not a proposition of fact relating to associations. ... In any case it is submitted that the controversy has no legal significance.[42]

Most disputes are about words, but not merely about words. Williams might say of an assertion that there is a wild bull and not a tame cow in the neighbouring field, that it is simply an assertion of the speaker's determination to use the words 'wild' and 'bull' in a certain way. Nevertheless, the belief might well lead to a practical policy being adopted which is different from the one which would be pursued by a person who rejected the usage. As we have seen, a judge's attitude towards the question of group personality is likely to determine the way he treats a group. Austin Farrer has remarked in connection with this method of philosophising: 'Metaphysical argument may be the grand cause of logical mirage; but linguistic conjuring is unrivalled for vanishing tricks.'[43] Should corporations and other associations be liable for crimes which require *mens rea* and for torts which need a guilty intention? Should the former property of the Free Church of Scotland belong to one ecclesiastical group or to another? These are very practical questions, and it was issues such as these which principally concerned the 'realists'. Legal practice has changed during the last hundred years, and no one would today hold the fiction theory in its strict form. This is not to say, however, that there was *never* a real issue at stake. In a similar vein, H. L. A. Hart tells us that we should stop thinking of 'personality' as a set of qualities. All that group persons and individual persons have in common is the word 'person', signifying the determination of lawyers to deal with them for some purposes in a similar way.[44] But surely they are likely to have something else in common; if not, we are forced to conclude that lawyers behave in a quite haphazard way; in which case the whole discipline of jurisprudence is misconceived. No doubt there are cases when the only relation existing between two entities is a verbal one, but equivocation is the exception and not the rule. Groups are treated as persons in law because this corresponds to a social fact about groups; groups and individuals are treated as persons in law, because the way in which they act is in some respects similar. We do not, as a rule, even in law, call two things by the same name unless they have something in common.

The notion of real personality was perhaps the aspect of pluralist theory which was most harshly criticised. Earl Latham, for example, while being generally sympathetic to the ideas of Laski, Figgis and Cole, attacks the concept of group personality. He maintains that the pluralists, after having taken away personality from the state, err by bestowing personality upon other associations.[45] Yet many of the pluralists did not deny that the state has a personality; Gierke certainly did not deny personality to the state, nor did Laski. Some of Latham's other criticisms of political pluralism will be looked at in a later chapter. L. C. Webb accuses the pluralists of deducing the sociological idea of group life from the fact that groups have a legal personality. He writes as follows,

> The doll so perfectly articulated that it is mistaken for flesh and blood is a familiar theme of classical ballet. Something of the same sort of illusion gave rise to English political pluralism. The group person as it exists within the universe of the law is a creation of art, a fictitious person. The English political pluralists were persuaded that the group person was real in the sense of existing independently of legal art.[46]

As we have seen, the English pluralists did not argue back

from the fact that the courts recognise group persons to the reality of group life.[47] Quite the reverse; they argued that groups were social facts and that the law inadequately reflected the nature of group life, and ought therefore to be modified. The pluralists certainly believed that groups exist as entities independently of legal art, but they did not argue in the way Webb thinks they did. Webb also maintains that Figgis failed to understand 'the significance of the Companies Act of 1862 and of later legislation providing an easy means of incorporation for non-profit associations'.[48] Yet we have seen that the position of corporations was not very different from that of unincorporated bodies with respect to the question of *ultra vires* and the right to develop. If the Free Church of Scotland had been a corporation, there is little reason to believe that it would have been in a stronger position.

The pluralist writers did not deny that there should be some machinery for recognising groups as legal persons, as long as it is realised that this is a matter of recognising something that really exists, rather than of inventing something which does not exist. D. Lloyd seems to have believed that the realists denied the need for any kind of recognition.[49] We have already seen how Gierke wrote of associations that they 'recieve through legal recognition of their personality' that which corresponds to their real nature. 'Spectacles are to be had in Germany', declared Maitland,

> which, so it is said, enable the law to see personality wherever there is bodiliness, and a time seems at hand when the idea of 'particular creation' will be as antiquated in Corporation Law as it is in Zoology.[50]

Nevertheless the spectacles are necessary: some kind of procedure is needed for the recognition of associations. Figgis also asserted the need for such recognition.

We may perhaps best conclude this chapter by a brief summary of the pluralists' ideas about group personality. They insisted that within the community there are many associations of various kinds, often acting with a kind of unity which allows us to use language normally reserved for describing the activities of individuals. Furthermore, the actions of groups cannot meaningfully be reduced to the actions of their individual members. Through the interaction of the individual members of the group new ideas are evolved and the group moves in new directions. These sociological facts ought to be recognised by the law, if we wish the law to remain an effective and realistic instrument of social control. These groups do not derive their social existence from being recognised as legal persons; rather they ought to be recognised as legal persons because they are social entities. The courts should also recognise the right of groups to develop and grow, and thus to modify their original purpose. These were some of the substantial points which the pluralist writers made about group personality, and they form one of the foundation stones upon which their political theory was based.

5 The State, the Group and the Individual

In the preceding discussion I have maintained that the pluralists based their political theory on a foundation of three pillars: a denial of state sovereignty, a belief that liberty is best preserved by a dispersion of power, and some notion of the 'real personality' of groups. The present chapter is concerned with their theories of the state, and with their ideas about the proper relationship between the state, the group and the individual. Before examining the theories of the state held by the leading pluralists of the period, I shall, however, glance briefly at the notions of the state against which the pluralists were reacting.

Many of the world's leading political philosophers have regarded groups as either irrelevant to political theory or, if relevant, then grudgingly to be recognised as significant but unwelcome intruders on to the political stage. Politics has often been seen as essentially a matter of the individual versus the state. An obvious example is Thomas Hobbes. Groups do not play an important part in his theory, although they are not ignored. In chapter 21 of *Leviathan*, he divided groups into two kinds: regular and irregular, and exhibited grave doubts about the positive value of either. He found it necessary to accept the family, but he objected to what we would call political parties, describing them as 'cabals' or 'factions'; lawful systems are thought of as in some ways analogous to muscles in the human body, while unlawful ones are like 'wens, biles and apostems'. Yet he regarded corporations as tending to the dissolution of the commonwealth, and if there were a large number of them in existence they were like 'worms in the entrails of a natural man'. In Rousseau's system, to take another example, groups were thought to break up the unity of the state, and to that extent were harmful. If the general will is perfectly to express itself, individuals are to be members of no partial societies or groups within the state, and each man must think as an isolated individual citizen.

For a final example from the school of individualist thinkers we shall take the prophet of late-nineteenth-century English rationalism, Henry Sidgwick. Cambridge was very much influenced by what Sidgwick said and thought, and he was a living influence there at the time Figgis wrote. In *Elements of Politics* he dealt with the relationship between voluntary societies and the state. The whole tone is one of suspicion towards groups; they are assumed to be potentially dangerous, and the author's aim seems to be to discover a means of suppressing as many of them as possible without violating the canon of individual liberty. 'Minor fragments' of governmental power can occasionally be conferred upon corporation and groups,[1] but generally speaking they are thought of as private rather than public institutions and exist strictly by permission of the state. Groups increase the danger of 'obstinate and systematic disobedience to Government'; the more force a 'recalcitrant element' can rely upon, the more the peril of disorder, though he graciously allows that 'this is not a decisive argument for discouraging such associations'. Groups constitute a great danger to the individual whom they are liable to coerce,[2] though the state should not necessarily intervene in all cases to stop this. Unlike Hobbes, he thought that a large number of religious bodies was less dangerous to the state than one single church. Religious groups provided a special problem for Sidgwick. The results which religious bodies achieved were thought by him to be in general useful, and for various reasons the state would find it inexpedient to take them over. So the state must get the church, or churches, into its power by offering various bribes, and the state should attempt to gain control of the finances of churches. Bequests to religious organisations are

liable to supply a dangerously strong inducement to the conscious or semi-conscious perpetuation of exploded errors, which, without this support, would gradually disappear.[3]

This somewhat quaint example of individualist collectivism which Sidgwick stood for is relevant for our purpose, as this was just the kind of political theory against which the pluralists strove.

In the late nineteenth and early twentieth century the most influential political philosophers in Britain were inspired by the idealist philosophy of Hegel. Writers like T. H. Green, B. Bosanquet and Henry Jones derived certain of their ideas from Rousseau, and they believed that the notion of a general will could be applied to the large nation state. They realised, however, that this meant recognising the important role which groups play. At this point it was Hegel who helped them most. Sociologically we must call Hegel a pluralist. Civil society, according to him, was made up, not primarily of individuals, but of groups, the existence of which binds together individuals in the larger unity of the state; it is only through the existence of groups that a dangerous atomism can be avoided. The weakness of the French system of government was, according to Hegel, partly due to the virtual absence of such associations. He was critical of the tendency to concentrate power in the central government, attacking that illiberal jealousy which attempts to suppress the freedom of subordinate groups in society to arrange their own affairs.[4] He insisted that 'dissimilarity in culture and manners is a necessary product as well as a necessary condition of the stability of modern states'.[5] Hegel, thus, believed in diversity in society, and maintained that national defence is the only thing which must in all circumstances be controlled by the central government. Although Hegel insisted that the interests of groups and associations 'must be subordinated to the higher interests of the state'[6], he did not mean by this that they must necessarily be subordinated to the interests of the central government, but to the common interest of the whole people. Green also saw that the national state can exist only on the basis of other forms of community life; it was for him 'the society of societies'. Bosanquet too recognised that, generally speaking, the affairs of society are carried on by persons arranged in groups. All these writers admitted the possibility that the central government might on certain occasions be in the wrong, and that some other group might be right. Was not Hegel recorded as speaking of 'the heavenly Antigone, the most glorious figure ever to have appeared on earth' — Antigone who is the personification of civil disobedience? And did not Green urge that in certain situations there is a positive duty to disobey? Nevertheless it is true that Hegel and his English disciples did believe that politics consists in the search for a common good in which the true interests of all individuals and associations would be included. 'The idealists' have had many critics, and have been accused of propagating a variety of conflicting errors. Earl Latham is apparently under the impression that 'the idealists' (which idealists?) postulated the state 'as a colossus of unity, a monolith, an absolute, a total system swallowing and assimilating all personal beliefs, attachments, obligations, and relations'.[7] From what has been said above, we may conclude that Latham is talking alarmist nonsense here.

In spite, however, of the pluralist element in the thought of many of the idealist writers on politics, G. D. H. Cole felt that as a pluralist he was living in a generally hostile climate in the first decades of the twentieth century. 'The whole tendency of nineteenth century philosophy', he wrote,

> was to regard the association as, at the most, a necessary imperfection, to be tolerated rather than recognised, with no rights beyond those of expediency, and no powers beyond those conferred expressly by statute. From this point of view we are now struggling slowly back to a saner doctrine.[8]

Pluralist writers like Figgis argued that the state is, as a fact, composed of a number of associations and groups, and that failure to recognise this will lead to disaster. Men are by nature social, and their interests are plural. Any attempt by the central government to suppress all groups will lead to resistance and eventually to violent upheaval. A wise government will not, therefore, attempt to eradicate group life. Pluralist writers also believed that a multiplicity of groups was beneficial to the state; that associations should be encouraged because (a) active participation in group life on the part of the individual leads to a healthy development of human personality, and (b) lively groups provide a bulwark against the totalitarian state. But how precisely did these pluralist writers see the state in its relationship with other groups and associations? It will become clear that there is no generally agreed theory of the state among these English political pluralists; furthermore it is sometimes difficult to discover a coherent view in the writings of any single thinker. Cole in particular tended to write too much and too rapidly; he seems very often to have published the first half-baked idea which came into his head.

I shall begin by looking at Figgis's view of the state. For him the state is a group which is composed of groups, rather than of individuals. The individual is a member of the state, according to this view, *through* his membership in subordinate associations. So the state is a community of communities, and it has a formal structure which culminates in the central government. The term 'state' is used by Figgis (a) to mean the collectivity of groups forming a single political entity, and also in a narrower sense (b) to mean the formal organs of government by which the collectivity acts as a single entity. A. D. Lindsay also accepted the notion of the state as an 'organisation of organisations'. It is because he thought of the state as a community of communities that Figgis could write of churches *in* the modern state rather than churches *and* the modern state, as one critic says he should have done.[9] The state is not, as it is with Laski, MacIver and even in some places with Maitland, merely another group, alongside economic, cultural and ecclesiastical groups. It is the community of communities, whose prime duty it is to maintain order among its members. H. M. Magid criticises Figgis's theory of the state as a *communitas communitatum*, arguing that his view that men are concerned with the affairs of the state only in so far as they are citizens, implies that the state is 'a *communitas* of the citizens for the regulation of the *communitates*'.[10] This criticism, however, ignores the oft repeated view of Figgis that men are members of the state only *through* their membership of societies like the church, the trade union or the family. Figgis normally used the term 'society' to refer to any one of the particular groups which compose the state. He did not therefore make that distinction between state and society which one recent author believes to be fundamental to political pluralism.[11] In fact, Figgis did not see the totality of groups which make up the state as constituting anything like a single society. The only thing binding this collectivity together is the civil or political bond. We do not therefore find Figgis writing of the personality of the state, as Laski did; the state was, for him, a very different kind of association from the trade union, the church or the sports club, which are bound together by a common purpose. The state exists simply to maintain some kind of order among contending groups.

Figgis insisted that it was the function of the state to regulate and to control the life of its member groups. But first of all the state must have some machinery for recognising groups. The state has to play an active role in deciding which group it should recognise as valid expressions of social life. The recognition of the legal personality of the individual citizen does not raise any great problems for the state, but the recognition of the legal personality of groups demands a more positive role for the state. However strongly we may believe in the naturalness of groups life, he asserted, it is the duty of the state to demand proper guarantees that a permanent group is being formed; furthermore, he maintained,

> it must clearly be within the province of the State to prevent bodies of persons acting secretly, and practically as corporations, in order to escape the rightful government control.[12]

If it is going to control the groups successfully, the state must require certain marks of group personality, such as registration, before it recognises the personality of associations. The job of the state is to maintain a situation in being where groups can pursue their several purposes as far as may be; conflict will arise, and in order to cope with these conflicts the state must have some machinery for registering and recognising groups. Although the state can withdraw recognition from a group, it cannot, in the nature of things, destroy a group. A group may continue to exist, and to manifest a social personality, even though it is unrecognised or even banned by the government. The group might indeed die, partly as a result of the withdrawal of state recognition, or if all its members were killed, but it is not created or destroyed by the state. This may seem like a mere quibble over words, but the point which Figgis was trying to emphasise was that groups do not owe their existence to state recognition. The state recognises groups because they exist; they do not derive their existence from being recognised. The christian church existed for centuries without such recognition, and yet remained a social entity with a personality.

As we have noted, Figgis insisted that although groups have rights, these are not absolute rights. He praised the puritans of the seventeenth century for denying that all rights were derived from the civil power, and asserting the right of religious groups to exist in the state.[13] Groups have rights, but not unlimited and absolute rights. The state exists

> to control and limit within the bounds of justice, the activities of all minor associations whatsoever. The point at issue is not whether Churches can do anything they choose, but whether human law is to regard them as having inherent powers, rights, and wills of their own — in a word, a personality. If they have, their activity might be restrained in so far as it interferes with others — thus, they would not be allowed to persecute, and ought not to be allowed.[14]

The state does not create the groups, but recognises and controls them; they have, so far as they are permanent, a personality and inherent rights. 'Is the civil society,' he demanded,

> a single power from which all rights proceed by delegation? In this case there is no real check upon tyranny, however democratic the form of government. Or is the state merely the final bond of a multitude of bodies, Churches, trade unions, families, all possessing inherent life, a real thing, recognized and regulated by the government, but no more the creation of its fiat, than are individual persons?[15]

Just as the right of the individual to do what he likes is limited, so is that of groups; they are more powerful than individuals, and there is always the danger of their demanding more than is just. The more exalted the object of the group, the more likelihood there is of its getting out of hand, and the greater is the need of governmental control.

Thus the main job of the state is to reconcile conflicting claims made by its members, allowing them as much scope for development and expression as is possible within the limits of order and peace. To control the groups, 'a strong power above them is needed' and it is largely in order to regulate such groups and keep them in order that the coercive force of the state exists. In another place he wrote of 'the Christian idea of the State as the controlling power', which guides but does not create groups.[16]

Thus, for Figgis, as for Dewey,[17] the state controls but does not create groups and individuals. He was opposed to a conception of an omnipotent state set against a mass of individuals who are its members — ' "the great leviathan" made up of little men, as in Hobbes's title-page'.[18] St Thomas Aquinas, he observed,

> does not make that cardinal error of political arithmetic, which sets the State on one hand against the mass of individuals on the other; but in his strong regard for the family and other social unions he regards the individual as belonging to the State, although he belongs to smaller social unions which exist in their own right and not by the mere fiat of an autocrat.[19]

Figgis believed that individualism and collectivism were but different sides of the same coin; a political atomism which sees society simply as a collection of isolated individuals leads very easily to the doctrine of an omnipotent state. 'The truth is', he declared, 'that both the State and the individual as commonly envisaged are not facts but fictions.'[20] Any attempt to base a system of politics upon these fictions is, he thought, sure to lead to anarchy or tyranny in the end.

One place where Figgis's theory is not sufficiently detailed is on the question of the extent to which the state is justified in intervening in the affairs of a group to prevent the persecution of individuals, or to maintain justice; he does not seem to have been fully aware of what Dicey called 'the paradoxical character' of the right of association.[21] He would certainly have said that the presumption is always that the individual has freely chosen to join the group, and however absurd its rules may appear to the outsider, the state should not, under normal circumstances, intervene. It can do so, though, when there is definite evidence of persecution. As the whole purpose of politics is thought to be the development of character by encouraging the faculty of free choice, there must be occasions when the character of individuals is being warped by a group to which they belong; should the state intervene to protect them? Figgis does not tell us on what occasions this might be justified. Presumably he would allow the state to stop corruption and fraud, and he stated more than once that it must have the final word on matters of property.

Inherent rights of groups are not absolute rights. We have already discussed the right of self-development which Figgis thought should be secured to groups. What other rights should groups possess? They should be allowed to exercise certain rights over their members, while they remain members (and the state should make sure that people are free to leave groups when they wish to). Figgis laid considerable emphasis on the right belonging to a family of supervising the up-bringing of children. Are we, he demanded, to have a system in which 'there shall be no intermediary between the State and the child', and where 'the claims alike of the religious body and of the family are to be set aside or rather denied?'[22] Is the state to recognise only individuals in this matter of education, and to ignore the corporate claims of groups? He objected to undenominationalism in religion because it attempts to do away with the church, and to consider only individuals. 'What', he demanded,

> is the real objection to undenominationalism? . . . It means the denial of religion except as an individual luxury or a State boon. . . . The only home is the State. The State is to consider individuals only — and in no way to recognise churches for the educational period of the great majority of its citizens.[23]

As Mandell Creighton had pointed out in a previous decade, the church wants nothing more than a guarantee that church parents should have the rights to give their children a church education; and 'The same liberty which we ask for ourselves we ask for all others.'[24] In addition to these rights a group should be allowed to determine the basis of its membership and to expel those who violate this basis. A free political community does not demand that individuals of whatever opinions should have the right of joining any group which they choose to join; there must be freedom for the group too — freedom to exclude those who violate its rules. 'The hopeless confusion of thought,' he wrote,

> between the right of the individual to choose for himself and his right to remain in a society pledged to one thing while he himself is pledged to the opposite would be incredible were it not so widespread, and would be the death-blow of all the political clubs that ever existed.[25]

Figgis was particularly concerned to establish the right of religious groups to excommunicate or to expel members whose actions or expressed beliefs put them out of sympathy with the purpose for which the group exists; he maintained that the group itself should be the judge of these matters.

Laski accepted much of what Figgis wrote on the relationship between the group and the state. Yet there are certain significant differences between them. Instead of seeing the state as a peculiar kind of group — itself composed of societies — Laski seems to have regarded the state as just one among many groups in 'society'. 'The state', he wrote, 'is only a species of a larger genus.' We must therefore distinguish clearly between state and society; the allegiance of men to the state is, he asserted, less important than their allegiance to 'society as a whole'.[26] It is not at all clear, however, what this latter term refers to. What is the nature of this 'society' to which men owe allegiance? What are the interests which bind it together? What are the relationships existing between its members?

As we have noted in a previous chapter, Laski maintained that the state has a personality, just as any other group has a personality. In the early twenties Laski's individualism forced him to modify these ideas about the personality of groups, and about the 'group will' which they were thought to possess. This will is nothing more than a number of individual wills acting in concert to achieve an agreed set of objects. The unity is not in the wills, but in the common object willed. And so there is nothing mysterious about the state; it is simply a group of men acting to realise a common purpose. 'One says America when one means a particular group of persons.'[27] A theory of the state, he maintained, is nothing more than a theory of the governmental act. He thus envisaged this group of men working together in a close way, accepting common aims and objectives, so that he could still use the concept of personality to apply to it. This leads us to ask about the nature of this common objective which the state pursues. At times he wrote of the state as a 'great public service corporation' having a limited but important welfare function. On other occasions he saw a much more glorious role for the state; ideally it should be concerned with 'the highest life for its members'. In these writings the hands are often the hands of Léon Duguit, but the voice is unmistakably that of T. H. Green. Laski became more and more convinced, however, that whatever the ideal may be, the state as it actually exists in a capitalist society operates in such a way as to secure the interests of a section of the community only. Even in his early writings, he had maintained that the real source of authority in a state is with those who hold economic power, and he insisted that what confronts us is 'a complex of interests; and between not a few of them ultimate reconciliation is impossible'.[28] Nevertheless Laski's doctrine of the state, as an ideal, implies a belief in the possibility of a common good, or a general will, representing the interests of the whole society, rather than those of the governmental clique. It has in fact been suggested that Laski's pluralism was partly the result of his belief that power in the liberal capitalist state of his day was in the hands of a small class; pluralism would do something to 'neutralise' the power of the state and thereby of that class.[29]

It is clear from this discussion how Laski was compelled to abandon the pluralist ideas which he had held in his early years, and to embrace a marxist notion of the state. If there is no common interest in a country, the state, conceived of as a body which is concerned with securing the highest life for all members of society, can have no purpose, and without a common purpose it cannot exist as a social entity at all. But in fact states do exist, and they do have a common interest binding them together; but it is the interest of the ruling class, whose aim it is to maintain a capitalist society in being, and to maintain their own position within it.

In chapter three I concluded that Laski believed the state to lack the power always to impose its will upon other groups, and that he further believed that it is usually unwise of the state to attempt to do so. In addition, groups possess certain rights which would make it immoral as well as unwise for the state to interfere with their activities, in so far as these do not affect the rights of other groups or individuals. Yet Laski refused to enter a detailed discussion of the respective spheres of the state, the group and the individual, arguing that this should be left to 'the test of the event'[30], whatever this may mean. From his discussion of certain legal and political issues, like the *Free Church of Scotland* case, the *Taff Vale* decision, the *Kulturkampf* in Germany and the secularist movement in France, we may gather that he advocated a considerable degree of freedom for the group. With respect to economic life, he envisaged a devolution of industrial power to functional groups, which would have authority to determine matters relevant to their particular industry; this had already happened to a considerable extent in the medical and legal professions. Democracy ought, he held, to be extended from the political to the industrial field. Workers should be given a real voice in the choosing of management. He further believed that there should be set up a federal council of producers to regulate industrial and economic matters, along the lines recommended by some of the guild socialists. Laski nevertheless concluded in his *Grammar of Politics* that adjudication by an assembly based upon universal suffrage and upon geographical representation was 'the best method of making final decisions in the conflict of wills within the community'.[31]

It is necessary to refer briefly to the ideas of G. D. H. Cole, and to try to unravel some of the confusions and contradictions in his theories of the state. The central theme running through Cole's early writings is an insistence that 'the various industries and services ought to be democratically administered by those who work in them'.[32] But the trouble began when Cole tried to put forward some theory about the relationship which should obtain among these groups, and between groups and individual citizens. The state was seen as being distinct from society, and as but one of the many associations within society; it is no more than the first among equals. The state is the organised machinery of government, and in the democratic countries of his day it rested upon the consent of men, secured on the basis of geographical representation. The state had in the past, according to Cole, made claims to exercise three kinds of function: economic, political and co-ordinational. He argued, however, that the state can properly concern itself only with those things which affect all members of the community in an equal way. With respect to economic functions, there are, he maintained, two aspects: consumption and production. The state can rightly act as a regulator of the former, but not of the latter. It is not at all clear why Cole thought that matters of consumption affect all men equally, while questions of production affect men differently. All men do not consume the same amount of brandy, and some people abjure its use entirely.[33] By the political function of the state Cole meant the regulation of personal relationships in society, and he appears to have believed that this is a valid function of the state. Finally he denied that the state could properly perform the role of co-ordination; it could not justly act as the adjudicator and adjustor of relationships between associations for the simple reason that, being itself an association of consumers, it would often have to act as judge in its own cause. He held a Rousseauite view of the sovereignty of the people, which cannot fully be represented by any association, and certainly not by the state. Nevertheless he did believe that a federal body, in which the state and other functional associations would be represented, would be able 'to speak in the name of our Sovereign',[34] and would act as the co-ordinator in a guild socialist society. He might just as well have said that the state should have a functional assembly, as well as an assembly based upon geographical representation, and then act as co-ordinator.

Bertrand Russell agreed with the majority of pluralist writers that the state should act as the co-ordinator and controller of groups. With Laski and Cole, he believed that the contemporary state acted, in practice, in the interests of a particular class and 'is largely concerned in defending the privileges of the rich'.[35] He argued that the positive purposes of the state should as far as possible be conducted by independent organisations rather that by the state itself, and that the state should concentrate upon maintaining order:

> There ought to be a constant endeavour to leave the more positive aspects of government in the hands of voluntary organizations, the purpose of the State being merely to exact efficiency and to secure an amicable settlement of disputes, whether within or without its own borders. And with this ought to be combined the greatest possible toleration of exceptions and the least possible insistence upon uniform system.[36]

Russell maintained that the theory of democracy demands more than majority rule; it requires the division of the community into more or less autonomous groups, which should have the right to determine those matters which affect their members only. Actions of groups which are likely to have direct effects upon non-members should be regulated by the state.[37]

The pluralist writings of Maitland, Figgis, Laski, Cole, Russell, Lindsay and others certainly amounted to a vigorous attack upon the sovereignty of the state, and on the wide claims for the state which were being made in many liberal and socialist circles. Ernest Barker was able to write in 1915 that 'the State has generally been discredited in England'.[38] It is true that the pluralist theories involved an attack upon certain doctrines of the state. From the preceding discussion, however, it is clearly nonsense to talk of the pluralists' 'studied disregard of the state', as Adam Ulam does.[39] Some of them may well be criticised for an incoherent and shifting view of what the state ought to do, but they certainly did not disregard it. Ulam further assumes that pluralism implies the rejection of state regulation of groups. This, as we have seen, is untrue of most of the pluralist writers. Cole is the only one of the writers whom we are considering in this essay who specifically denied that the state ought to regulate and control the groups; yet he invented a federal body to do the job. The other writers thought that the specific function which distinguished the state from other groups is that of regulation and control. What they denied was that the state is infallible; there may be occasions when groups and individuals ought to resist the commands of the state. It may be said that this opens the gate to anarchy. Laski grasped the nettle firmly and admitted that 'at the root of our social system there is a contingent anarchy',[40] for the group and the individual can never properly hand over to the state their rights of resisting unjust laws. Figgis had made the same point:

> The only way to be sure an individual will never become a criminal is to execute him; the only way to secure a State from all danger on the part of its members is to have none. Every State is a synthesis of living wills. Harmony must ever be a matter of balance and adjustment, and this at any moment might be upset, owing to the fact that man is a spiritual being and not a mere automaton.[41]

I have observed in a previous section that many of the idealist political theorists were pluralists of a kind. They recognised the importance of social groups in the state. The pluralists, for their part, were not all philosophical pluralists, and even those who were did not accept the kind of ethical pluralism which denies the possibility of any right action by an individual in a given situation, resolving the individual into a number of 'roles'. How then did these pluralist writers differ from the Hegelians? They agreed that in an ideal situation the commands of the state would not conflict with the legitimate purposes of the groups, and that the individual would not be faced with a conflict in loyalties. But the pluralists denied that this total situation could ever be embodied institutionally in a single organ — the state. Perhaps the most interesting criticisms of political pluralism came from Miss M. P. Follett in her book *The New State*. She argued that the pluralists were under the mistaken impression that unity involves absorption, whereas a true unity takes

differences into account and transcends them by including
them in a higher unity. This ultimate unity is the state, in its
idea. The state is composed of individuals, and this ideal state
'demands the whole of me'; 'the home of my soul', she
declared, 'is in the state'.[42] In an article published some
months after her book, Miss Follett maintained that the
pluralists had based their theory on 'a non-existent individual'.[43] There can never be a situation where the individual
has to choose between loyalty to a group and loyalty to the
state; anyone who thinks otherwise ignores the time factor,
and forgets that community is 'a process'. There is, she
insisted, no individual who stands outside and looks at his
groups. Whether the person stands outside or not is doubtful,
but the pluralist writers were surely correct in believing that
he is forced on numerous occasions to make a choice between his loyalty to his church or trade union, and the
demands of the state. This is just the kind of decision which
workers often have to make when their union calls a strike; it
is the kind of decision which churchmen have to make when
a government passes laws which they believe to be inconsistent with the rights of their church. Vivid examples of this
kind of conflict can be seen in a little book edited by H.
Gollwitzer called *Dying We Live;* in this book the case of
C. F. Goerdeler, who put the interests of his city above what he
regarded as the unjust claims of the state, is particularly
relevant. Miss Follett was clearly wrong when she asserted
that a person's loyalty to a particular group can never
conflict with demands made by the state. She used as evidence the fact that a man can vote for one thing at a branch
meeting of his trade union today, and for a party which
opposes this policy tomorrow. This is, of course, true, but it
is not evidence for the assertion that the individual can never
be faced with a moral problem of having to choose. He may
in this particular instance be acting irrationally, or he may
have changed his mind about the merits of the policy in
question, or he may have voted for the party in spite of its
labour policy, or the situation may have changed overnight.
But in certain cases of this kind the individual is most
assuredly faced with a moral problem, and is obliged to act as
far as possible in a rational and consistent manner. In her

book, however, Miss Follett seems to have been arguing merely that in the *ideal* situation the individual would not have to make these decisions — that in a 'true federalism' these problems ought not to arise. 'We should not', she wrote, 'be obliged to choose between our different groups'.[44] With this the pluralists would have had no quarrel.

Adam Ulam makes the same kind of criticism when he states that 'the dichotomy between the state and other social groups is as unreasonable as the one between the individual and the state'.[45] By 'dichotomy' Ulam obviously does not mean classificatory distinction; no one could possibly deny that there is such a useful classificatory distinction between the individual and the state, and most of the pluralists insisted on a classificatory distinction between the state and other groups (though, as we have seen, Laski did not). By 'dichotomy' he must mean antagonism. The pluralists would have agreed that in an ideal situation there would be no such antagonism, but in the world as we find it, anyone who denies the possibility and indeed the likelihood of such an antagonism frequently manifesting itself is politically illiterate.

A more valid criticism of these pluralist writers would be that they failed to take seriously the challenge to individual freedom which might come from the group itself, and therefore hardly considered the criteria according to which the state might properly intervene in the internal affairs of a group to secure the rights of individual members. In general they believed that so long as the individual was formally free to leave the group, then any discipline to which he submitted was voluntary and not a matter with which the state should interfere. But there may be economic and social pressures which make it practically impossible for the individual to leave the group, and in this situation the only hope for the individual might be some kind of interference from outside. What is more, if the ultimate purpose of the state is to allow for and encourage the development of human character, may it not be the case that there are certain groups whose ways of life and systems of belief cramp or cripple the characters of their members and which ought therefore to be interfered with by the state? The answer of the pluralists to this was that as a general rule this kind of interference causes more harm than good, and therefore ought not to be encouraged. J. S. Mill insisted that the state should never interfere with an adult civilised person for his own good; the pluralists adapted this dogma and applied it to the group: the state should not interfere with the life of a group for the good of the group itself (or for the good of its individual members). Ultimately the bad consequences of this kind of interference would outweigh the advantages. We return to this problem in the next chapter.

A further criticism needs to be considered. It may not always be true that powerful groups are successful bulwarks against tyranny. By making an alliance with the leaders of the most powerful groups in the state the potential tyrant might be able to exercise a degree of social control which otherwise would be difficult to achieve. The machinery for such control is ready-made, and needs simply to be taken over by the aspiring tyrant. If he is able to enlist the support of the leaders of well organised groups he might be saved the bother of exercising direct control over large numbers of citizens; much of this might be done for him by the group leaders. Yet these leaders will represent a continual threat to the tyrant's position unless he is able swiftly to replace them with persons selected by himself. Tightly controlled, hierarchically organised, well-disciplined groups may be a more formidable bulwark against the pretensions of a tyrant whose policies they reject than are loosely organised and less disciplined groups, but the former are potentially of more use to the tyrant once he is able to secure control of them. Opposition from the Roman Catholic Church may have been one of the principal factors in destroying the Peron government in Argentina and the Trujillo regime in the Dominican Republic, but on other occasions this church has been a bastion of tyrannical regimes, and one of their principal instruments of control. In the early years of the Duvalier regime, the church in Haiti was one of the most important centres of opposition to the claims and aims of the government; but once its hierarchy was changed in accordance with the wishes of the president, the church has become a more or less docile, but effective, instrument in the hands of the government.[46]

6 Authority in the Church

The question of authority within associations and groups is distinct from that of authority in the state, but the two are closely connected. In the first place, Figgis, Laski, Cole, and the other writers with whom we are principally concerned in this book, argued that the pluralist state is justified ultimately by the likelihood that it will maximise individual freedom, they cannot therefore totally ignore the possible threat to this freedom which might emanate from the groups which compose such a state. Pluralists might otherwise justifiably be accused of handing over the individual from one tyranny to another. Secondly, it is likely that many of the arguments which the pluralists used against a concentration of power in the state will apply to the large associations which are found within the state. A recent American writer has distinguished between the 'pluralist' — 'arguing for the autonomy of the private association from the absolutism of the state' — and the 'liberal pluralist' — who insists also on 'the independence of the individual from the absolutism of the group'.[1] Other contemporary American writers generally sympathetic to the pluralist position have warned against the danger of group tyranny. Philip Selznick observes that 'the private organisation can be more oppressive than the state',[2] and goes on to consider ways in which legal ideals can be applied to the group life of the modern state. Small voluntary groups are able to evolve a democratic and participatory form of internal government, but once groups acquire a sizable administrative staff, and once they develop what Selznick calls 'a dependent constituency', the situation is likely to change. The bureaucrats become the central feature of the organisation and the members become mere clients. The voluntary nature of the association is eroded as systems of private taxation and various types of sanction are introduced and 'as the effective enterprise, carried forward by the administrative organization, gains the capacity to perpetuate its existence'.[3] It is therefore not out of place in the present volume to take the problem of authority and power in the church, as viewed by one of the leading pluralist writers, as a case study in the more general problem of the internal government of groups in a pluralist state.

Like Joseph de Maistre in the previous century, Figgis saw the problem of authority in the church as analogous to that of authority in the state. '*Infallibility* in the spiritual order, and *sovereignty* in the temporal order', declared the French ultramontane,

> are two words perfectly synonymous. Each expresses that high power which dominates all others, from which all others derive, which governs and is not governed, which judges and is not judged . . . because all government is absolute.[4]

Figgis insisted that ideas of state sovereignty were closely linked to false views about authority in the church, and he traced the way in which the civilian doctrine of the emperor as the source of all law had been applied in the church. 'That notion of authority', he wrote,

> which reaches its limit in Ultramontanism is, at bottom, a false legalism, accepted from the antique city state, to which the individual was only a means, developed in the jurists' theory of the Roman law, and transferred during the course of the Middle Ages from the civil power to the ecclesiastical.[5]

It was this ultramontane theory, rather than the idea of the papacy in itself, to which he objected. The ultramontane's idea of authority is absolute and oracular, and the church is seen as a monolithic unit 'with all power centred in the Pope or derived from him, and no jurisdiction nor any rights existing except expressly or tacitly by his delegation'.[6] This theory holds that all authority is derived from the centre in precisely the same way that the theory of sovereignty derives all civil rights of groups and of individuals from the state. As a result, episcopal authority is unduly depressed, as the jurisdiction of each bishop is held to emanate from Rome, and bishops and priests become mere delegates of the pope.[7] Figgis agreed with George Tyrrell that the ultramontane idea of authority was as individualistic as that of the protestant sectarian. 'They have many Popes,' remarked Tyrrell, 'we but one'.[8]

Authority is a phenomenon which is manifested in all established groups and is, according to Figgis, an expression of the social nature of man.[9] Within the church, authority ought not to be seen in terms of a set of officials giving orders to the rank and file members, and it is quite wrong to think of laypeople as basins into which the truth is to be poured.[10] Figgis attacked clericalism in the church, and insisted that laypeople share in the authority of the church. 'All alike share it,' he wrote, 'all in some way submit to it; and all contribute to it'.[11] An individual can recognise the authority of a body to which he belongs and generally agree to abide by its rules without seeing it as alien and entirely external to himself, nor need he regard this authority as infallible.

There are, Figgis suggested, two principal bulwarks against ecclesiastical tyranny: the devolution of power and of decision-making to small groups within the church, and the ultimate supremacy of conscience. 'Within the Catholic society let there be groups as many as you will', he declared.

> We need more, not less, of the guild principle. So long as human life exists there will be temperaments in which the personal side of religion is uppermost; others which emphasise the critical; others the sacramental and institutional.[12]

These permanent and semi-permanent groups within the church have an inherent life which is not derived from the centre.[13]

Figgis saw the conciliar movement of the fifteenth century as a great and noble endeavour to achieve the ideal of a federal catholicism. The aim of Gerson, D'Ailly, Zabarella and others had been to reintroduce federal democracy into the church, to recognise the limited autonomy of national and provincial churches, and to regard final authority as belonging to the whole body rather that to a small group of officials headed by the pope; this final authority manifested itself in the form of a general council.[14] Figgis saw the failure of the conciliar movement as a tragedy for the western church, making reformation in a more drastic form almost inevitable. A later writer has remarked on the fact that the twentieth-century catholic would regard the existence of national churches as incompatible with the fact of a universal church. 'Yet the truth is', he went on, 'that the very same notion that sounds so shocking to many good Christians of our day had no terror for the early Christians'.[15] It was this general interest in the question of national churches which led Figgis to a study of Bossuet and Gallicanism.[16] Bossuet had opposed extreme papalist claims and had argued in favour of a limited autonomy for national churches. Febronianism can be seen as another example of this claim for limited national autonomy within the catholic church. Figgis noted other movements which had made similar claims.[17]

It was in this general context of federalism within the church that Figgis viewed the claims of the Church of England. 'We are standing up in England,' he wrote of the Anglican position,

> not only for individual freedom so much as for the reality of the group-life within the Church, for a conception of the religious society which is organic and federalised, as against one which is merely unitary and absolutist.[18]

Figgis emphasised the debt which the Anglican Church owed to Rome, and saw no reason why Anglicans should not be willing to accept the ideal of papal primacy in a unified church.[19] He even suggested that the doctrine of papal infallibility was susceptible of an interpretation which Anglicans might accept, 'just as the legal doctrine "the king can do no wrong" can be interpreted in a way favourable to freedom'.[20] While he defended the distinctiveness of the English church he insisted that it must be seen as part of a larger whole. 'The notion of absolute, independent entities must go,' he insisted, 'the national group is real, with its own real life, but it is a group, a part'.[21]

The second bulwark against ecclesiastical tyranny is the ultimate duty of the individual to follow his conscience, to do what he believes to be right, after he has considered the evidence and given due weight to the appropriate authorities. Figgis agreed with Newman in wishing to drink 'to Conscience first, and to the Pope afterwards'.[22] Yet he denied that individual conscience is to be seen as an authority in religion; it is rather the faculty for discriminating between authorities and for sifting the evidence. The Quaker idea of the 'inner light' as an authority in religion is not, Figgis argued, a christian one at all.[23] Nevertheless the christian faith should be preached in such a way as to find a genuine response in the individual conscience; it is not a list of propositions to be accepted on the basis of some external authority. 'Wherever blind obedience is preached,' he declared, 'there is danger of moral corruption'.[24]

While the individual ought ultimately to do what he believes to be right, a church must have the power to draw the line at some point and be able to expel those who transgress that line. We have already noted, in a previous chapter, the pluralist insistence that this power of exclusion be accorded to the group, otherwise it would be unable to perpetuate itself as a distinct group. Nevertheless Figgis was particularly concerned that this right should be exercised by church officials only when absolutely necessary, only, that is, when the gospel was being endangered or when the very life of the church was being threatened. At the time that Figgis was writing the Roman Catholic Church was going through the modernist crisis, and in the Anglican Church liberal protestantism was becoming influential. This raised problems of church discipline. When were the bishops justified in attempting to suppress such unorthodox opinions? On what occasions could an individual properly subscribe to articles and credal statements when he believed them, if at all, in a non-literal sense? Henry Sidgwick had advocated a strict interpretation, arguing that any subscription which was not based on a literal and total acceptance implied dishonesty. He had himself resigned his Cambridge fellowship rather than subscribing to beliefs which he could not accept.[25] A considerable debate ensued on this question, with bishops like Mandell Creighton and Charles Gore accepting the strict interpretation of Sidgwick, and theologians like Rashdall, Bethune-Baker, Gwatkin and Sanday arguing for a more liberal construction of subscription.[26] In the Roman Catholic Church writers like Acton, Tyrrell and many modernists had to face a similar problem. Tyrrell himself argued that as long as a liberal catholic,

> believes himself to be in communion with the spirit of the whole Church, he need not trouble himself about the views of her officers for the time being, unless in some matter obedience to them would put him in a false position.[27]

Lord Acton's predicament was somewhat the same.[28] It is only if you assume that official absolutism is of the essence of the church that liberal catholics can be condemned in their attitude to the question of conformity, and it is this very idea which they disputed. It was, Tyrrell argued, only by remaining where they were that the liberals can hope to break the grip of officialism.[29]

Although Figgis disagreed with Tyrrell on a number of issues, adopting a generally more conservative theological position, he strongly sided with the liberals on this matter. So long as a person believed that the church is the society for promoting the will of God and was prepared to accept the obligation to recite the creed as a minister in that society, it would be wrong to accuse him of dishonesty or disloyalty if his interpretation of the articles of the creed were not exactly that which was accepted by the hierarchy of the church. The church should not be confused with the hierarchy, nor should the catholic faith be equated with the current theological opinions accepted by this set of officials. A person does not cease to be British as soon as he criticises the government of the day, and 'cases there are like that of Athanasius, when the individual by his courage to stand alone, has saved the church'.[30] Figgis summed up his position on the question of loyalty and the ethics of subscription in the following words:

> Loyalty to the idea of the Church, to its living Lord, to its earthly membership, to its multitudinous life, to the many-coloured richness of its sanctity, to the romance of its origin, to the treasures of its present inheritance, but

above all loyalty to the splendour of its future glory; — that is the root of the matter. When a man feels that he has that, who are we that we should lightly charge him with dishonour, merely because he applies in one place methods of exegesis which each one of us applies elsewhere?[31]

This is not the place to examine in general the theological position adopted by Figgis, but he shows that it is quite possible to be theologically conservative and ecclesiastically liberal, just as the late bishop E. W. Barnes demonstrated the possibility of the reverse combination.

As we shall see in the next chapter, Figgis had come to the conclusion that churches in the England of his day must accept their position as voluntary groups in a secular state, nevertheless he was a fervent critic of 'sectarianism', in the theological sense of that term. He attacked puritanism for attempting to turn the church into a sect of like-minded people. Intellectualism in religion also tends to be oligarchic, while certain forms of mysticism, such as that of Fénelon, have an aristocratic tendency which is contrary to the catholic idea of the church.[32] The catholic position, on the other hand, allows for different types and levels of spirituality. 'The Church,' he insisted, 'is not meant to consist only of spiritual athletes, still less is it meant to consist of spiritual dilettanti'.[33] Although the Church of England should cease imagining that it is the religious side of the nation, it should continue to make an appeal to 'all sorts and conditions of men', and should avoid turning itself into a clique of respectable people concerned with cultivating their own souls. Some of the consequences of Figgis's attempt to combine sociological sectarianism with theological anti-sectarianism, thus challenging a basis thesis of Troeltsch,[34] will be considered in the following chapter.

The question of the structure of authority within the church has continued to be a vexed one, and it was one of the principal concerns of the Second Vatican Council. There have been significant developments in the Roman Catholic Church in recent years away from centralisation towards a more federal conception of the church. 'Why', demands one writer in the journal *Concilium*,

> did a Church which began as a loose assemblage of quasi-autonomous communities become a massive bureaucratic organisation with power and authority concentrated in the pope?[35]

He states that the principal causes of this centralising tendency have been 'defensive responses aimed at dealing with uncertainty and threat'.[36] In recent years national and regional churches in the Roman communion have acquired new powers and fresh initiative, and it has been suggested that institutions like the partriarchate might be revived as part of a move to decentralise.[37] Karl Rahner has argued also that there is to be found in the Roman Catholic Church today a pluralism in theological matters which is of a quite new kind. 'The quantitative increase in theological pluralism over the centuries', he writes, 'has produced, as it were, a qualitative mutation.'[38] In the past, he argues, there were disagreements, but theologians either 'shared the same terminology, philosophical presuppositions, speech world and outlook on life', or they did not explicitly recognise theological disagreements.[39] According to Rahner, one of the possible consequences of this lack of agreement on philosophical presuppositions and the accompanying theological pluralism is that the *magisterium* of the church will not in the future 'be able to formulate new emphatic doctrinal pronouncements'.[40] The principal reason for this inability is that such dogmatic pronouncements have to be made in the language of some theology, and there is today no such generally accepted language. The *magisterium* might then be restricted to setting limits to theological speculation from time to time, and to making occasional pastoral directives. When it does so, it will really be saying:

> You cannot talk like this in the Church without endangering your own faith or the faith of others and doing injustice to the doctrine involved.[41]

Professor Maurice Wiles has attempted to develop these ideas of Rahner. He argues that 'the newer approach' regards theology as 'inductive and empirical' and consequently as 'inadequate and provisional'.[42] There are no 'fixed criteria' for the determination of theological truth. Wiles therefore suggests that the church should be willing to tolerate 'a considerable measure' of what appears to be error, and to allow 'a wide range' of theological differences within her borders. With most of this Rahner could agree. But Wiles goes on to speak of the truth which is made known in Jesus Christ as 'something for which we have continuously to search', and criticises attempts to tie down speculation by ecclesiastical pronouncements.

> We need rather to be prepared to trust one another and to be ready to be at one with all those who are ready to be at one with us in the name of Christ.

Although Wiles manifestly believes that there must be some limit to theological speculation (as it is only a *considerable measure* and a *wide range* of disagreement which should be permitted) he gives no indication of the criteria for determining such limits. Rahner's position is quite different from that of Wiles. He clearly distinguishes the 'givenness' of the christian faith from the words in which it is expressed, seeing these as signposts which point to realities. 'These realities', he states, 'are mediated to us by words, but they are experienced as being present not absent'. The christian faith is 'a given datum totally independent of the problem posed by contemporary theological pluralism'.[43] We have already noted Rahner's belief that the church can properly set limits to theological speculation, and he explicitly denies that theological pluralism legitimates soft tolerance for everything and anything.[44] The position which Rahner maintains is similar to that for which Figgis had argued.

The question of authority and power within groups and associations is one which must concern the pluralist who bases his political theory upon the importance of liberty. It is likely that he will argue that a decentralised system of power, and a diffusion of authority throughout the group, are valuable, and that a concentration of power at one point is likely to lead to corruption, and to constitute a threat to the liberty of individual members of the group. Nevertheless this recognition by no means implies that the state should, as a general rule, intervene to secure this structure within groups. Such state action may well fail to achieve what is intended, and may have a number of unfortunate consequences. As Grant McConnell has pointed out, with respect to trade unions:

> If a strong external system of limitations is imposed on union power, the unions may lose much of their usefulness within the social system or their sense of grievance may be whetted to a dangerous edge. If extensive regulation of internal union affairs is legislated, the unions may become so debilitated that their subsequent survival will be a matter of indifference.[45]

Recent suggestions from the British Conservative Party that a particular form of election should be imposed upon the unions by statute are open to this sort of criticism. An attempt by the state to impose such a democratic system on hierarchically organised religious groups might be the sequel, and this would meet with considerable resistance.

7 Some Institutional Consequences of Pluralism

One of the consequences of political pluralism, particularly in the form advocated by J. N. Figgis, was an acceptance of the idea of a secular state. A particular church is merely one among many religious, non-religious and anti-religious groups in the state, and as such it can claim no special privileges. In medieval christendom there was very little conception of two distinct societies, the church and the state. The idea of church and state as two aspects of one great society was held by all medieval thinkers, even by anti-clerical writers like Marsilius; it was perpetuated in the post-reformation period, particularly among Anglican and Lutheran writers. 'With this view,' Figgis asserted, 'either an ecclesiastical or a civil tyranny is almost inevitable'.[1] He traced a new view to the Presbyterian and Jesuit writers of the sixteenth and seventeenth centuries, who, when in a minority, developed the idea of a church as one group in a plural state, in order to secure toleration for themselves. Among Anglican writers, from Thorndike through Stillingfleet to Warburton, he saw a growing awareness of the church as a distinct society; the Oxford Movement essentially involved the demand for spiritual independence for the church. As Laski observed, 'Tractarianism is essentially the plea of the corporate body which is distinct from the State to a separate and free existence'[2]; he saw Figgis's theory as 'the lineal successor to Pusey's tract on the royal supremacy'.[3]

Figgis insisted that all talk about a national church was, by the beginning of the twentieth century, misleading and dangerous. The Church of England was no longer co-extensive with the nation. Toleration, which as we have already noted, was achieved largely through the demands made by intransi-

gent religious minorities, had itself led to the multiplication
of sects. The only way to achieve a national religion would be
on the basis of a highest common factor of the religious
beliefs of the people; it would be a religion shorn of the
supernatural, and would end with 'the establishment and
endowment of the Pleasant Sunday Afternoon'.[4]

The nation was, then, no longer christian in any substantial
sense; this was the fact. But Figgis went on to argue that a
tolerant secular state, which admits the possibility of competing religious groups within it, is the best kind of state. The
state should allow religious groups to exist and to order their
own affairs without interfering; these groups should be able
to prescribe their creeds and must have the right to determine
the limits of their membership. But, in exchange, these
groups must not try to force upon the whole nation religious
practice or moral prohibitions which stem from their peculiar
beliefs. 'We cannot eat our cake and have it,' he wrote,

> We cannot claim liberty for ourselves, while at the same
> time proposing to deny it to others. If we are to cry 'hands
> off' to the civil power in regard to such matters as mar-
> riage, doctrine, ritual, or the conditions of communion
> inside the Church — and it is the necessary condition of a
> free religious society that it should regulate these matters
> — then we must give up attempting to dictate the policy of
> the State in regard to the whole mass of its citizens.[5]

When judging political questions we should do so as citizens,
and not as churchmen, remembering that many Englishmen
are not churchmen. As citizens, he maintained, christians
have no right to appeal to motives or ideals which are
specifically christian. It would be quite wrong for the church
to advocate a policy which is specifically christian in a
community which is heterogeneous in religion.[6] Figgis insisted that as clear a distinction between crime and sin, between
private morality and law, should be drawn as is possible. It
would, for example, be a mistake for the church to attempt
to impose upon the nation its own view of marriage, though
if it chooses to forbid its members to remarry after divorce
that is no business of the state.

Figgis did not advocate that christians should withdraw

from politics, and it would seem that his views would require the possibility of a secular morality, distinct from christian morality, which should be the concern of the state; the law should not necessarily forbid divorce, but it should certainly forbid murder. He believed that men can unite upon matters of political ethics who differ widely in their theology or in their metaphysics, and argued that the notion of a secular or plural state is one which, though demanded by christian ethics, could also be accepted by non-christians. But what is the nature of this secular morality which governs the actions of the state? Unfortunately, Figgis was not explicit on this matter. One possible answer would be that there is a natural law which is distinct from the revealed law; it is a law applying to all men because of their common humanity, being discoverable by means of reason, which is a common possession of all; natural law according to this view provides the basis of that common good which it is the duty of the state to realise. But Figgis did not believe that it was the function of the state to achieve some substantive common good for its members; this was to be achieved by those subordinate groups to which all men belong. The state should simply concentrate on maintaining in existence a situation where there should be as much freedom as possible for groups and individuals to pursue ends which they choose.

The more fundamental problem therefore concerns the ethical basis of this very theory of the state. Perhaps the basis is very wide, political pluralism may well be compatible with many ethical theories, but it is surely the case that it is incompatible with some ethical theories. Figgis's theory of a secular state assumes that christians and non-christians can agree on a broad political ethic, while disagreeing in their theological or metaphysical pictures of the world. The kind of politics we pursue or advocate certainly depends upon moral beliefs to which we subscribe, and our moral beliefs are often closely connected to our religious beliefs. I have endeavoured to show elsewhere[7] that political ends are not self-evident, and that politics is not an autonomous activity; it depends upon moral ideas. But is it possible to arrive at generally agreed moral ideas — a social ethic — which is unrelated to theological or metaphysical beliefs? J. F.

Stephen denied that you can reconcile the morals of Jesus
Christ with the theology of Julius Caesar, and Figgis seems to
have agreed with him. He praised Nietzsche for seeing 'that it
was hopeless to maintain the Christian standards apart from
the Christian faith'.[8] Discussing the period when Matthew
Arnold thought that christian morals could be retained while
dispensing with dogma, he wrote,

> Differences of creed have at length revealed a yawning
> chasm between our moral ideals. Apologists of those days
> were scorned as narrow-minded for venturing the view that
> Christian ethics were bound up with Christian dogma, and
> that with the decay of the one the other could not long
> maintain its hold. What they said, however, has come
> true.[9]

Might it not be the case that when he denied the likelihood
of retaining a christian morality after the theological foundation has been removed, Figgis was referring solely to individual morality? For one thing it is difficult to separate personal from social morality in this way, and he explicitly
stated that christian ethics 'form the only enduring basis of a
noble social life'.[10] If then our ethical ideals depend intimately on our theological beliefs, if scepticism in the one will lead
to corruption of the other, then the prospects of a secular
state can hardly be said to be hopeful. If indeed there is no
possibility of christians and non-christians agreeing on the
moral and political principles which lie at the basis of our
social life, how are we to ensure the future of that idea of the
state which we have called pluralist? If this pluralism does
rest upon a christian ethic, which in turn relies upon christian
dogma, what will happen to the state when the dogma is
no longer believed? Might it not be that if Figgis's theory of
the dependence of ethics on theology be true, then the worst
possible step for the church to take is the very one which he
advocated — the acceptance of its position as a mere sect? If
our social ethics depend upon belief in God, should not the
church continue to impose its theology upon the nation as a
whole as far as it can, to maintain and increase its control of
education, to attack the growth of secular thought with all
the weapons in its power? If Figgis really believed with

Mandell Creighton that it was a fallacy to hold 'that Christian ethics could stand by themselves apart from Christian doctrine',[11] should he not have accepted the 'christian nation' theory which Creighton also held, and rejected the secular state as disastrous? Alternatively, if he wished to accept the secular state, would it not have been more consistent to have adopted Lord Acton's more hopeful views on the possibility of a basically christian social ethic divorced from christian theology? If we deny God, Acton held, whole branches of deeper morality lose their sanction, yet an adequate system of social ethics can be maintained without recourse to theology. Acton's admiration for George Eliot was enormous, and the reason was quite as much moral as literary; she was for him the perfect atheist, and her writings demonstrated how it was possible to have morals without religion. For Acton, ethical theory was basic, and religious doctrines were to be judged mainly in terms of their moral content; religious differences do not necessarily imply a diversity of moral principles. With these ideas it is, of course, quite possible and legitimate to advocate a secular theory of the state, in which this non-theological morality could be assumed as the basis of a liberal politics. It therefore looks as though Figgis must sacrifice one of his masters, and it is most likely that he would have given up Creighton's idea rather than the concept of a secular state, and have argued for a minimum of ethical autonomy. It might indeed be said that, so far from good social ethics being the invariable companion of christian theology. immoral social doctrines like the duty of persecution have not only been held by christians but advocated on the grounds of their being christian; when the church has been politically influential and strong it has often been morally corrupt, thus it may be the case that christian morality can not only be held without christian dogma, but perhaps flourishes best when 'the church has to struggle to maintain its faith. Indeed, Figgis might himself be said to have recognised this in some of his writings. He thought that the effect on the church of the gradual secularisation of social life is by no means wholly bad. The church has lost in extension, but it has gained in intensity. Although the church is no mere sect of devout persons, much harm is

done by making christianity so wide that everyone is included whatever his beliefs; all we can hope for is a religion
which makes a universal appeal. 'There will be fewer', he told
a Cambridge congregation,

> that comes of liberty. For two hundred years religious
> freedom has been developing. With this, the proportion of
> any one religious body to the whole must be smaller.[12]

There does, thus, appear to be something of a confusion of
thought here though not a necessary contradiction. Figgis
might very well have replied that the prospects for the secular
state he advocated were certainly grim, but even worse would
be the situation if the church tried to maintain the old idea
of a christian commonwealth. The mass of people had become
dechristianised in spite of the church's clinging on to the old
notion; the church must acknowledge the secular state and
do the best it can in the situation. Christian theology has a
better chance of surviving when a vigorous church lives in a
secular state than when a flabby church exists as part of a
nominally christian commonwealth. He had little faith in
'diffused christianity'.

The theory of a secular state has continued to be a matter
of acute controversy in many countries. In the United States
there have been wide disagreements about the interpretation
of the constitutional provision which forbids the establishment of religion; symbolic issues like prayers in state schools
and the official use of the phrase 'In God we trust' have
revealed important theoretical disagreements about the
notion of a pluralist or secular state. In Italy there has been
much controversy centred on the problem of divorce. In
Britain the report of the Wolfenden Committee provoked an
extended debate about the relation of law to morality. The
chief participants in this 'splendid encounter' — 'courteous
and restrained'[13] — have been Lord Devlin and Professor
Hart.[14] The reason why such a charming confrontation is able
to take place is that both of the principal participants agree
on some of the more important issues at stake. They both
think that 'society' is bound together by a set of moral
beliefs; Hart appears to assume that there are some basic
beliefs common to all societies, while Devlin's view is that

some moral beliefs must be shared by the members of a society, though the content of these may vary from one society to another. They disagree about whether it is possible to delimit a sphere of private conduct which should not be subject to interference by the law. Devlin believes that in certain circumstances it is legitimate to enforce or attempt to enforce by law provisions of the current moral code of a country, and denies that it is possible to specify in advance a sphere of private conduct which should never be interfered with. Hart thinks that it is wrong for the state to attempt to enforce a moral code in matters where individual conduct will have no harmful consequences. But significantly they agree in rejecting J. S. Mill's principle that it is never right for society to interfere with the adult in a civilised nation for his own good; they both accept the legitimacy of paternalism. Mitchell says that they are both 'recognizably, liberals'[15]; it might be more true to say that they are both disguised totalitarians. They agree with Marx that legal institutions are part of the superstructure of society, and that it is the function of law to maintain in being the current arrangements of that society; though Hart makes provision for a sphere of private conduct which should be exempt from such legal interference.

Although Figgis's theories had no spectacular results, there are indications of a gradual adoption of his notion of a secular state. 'All students of the subject,' wrote a later author on church and state,

> must be consciously or unconsciously influenced in what they write by the many-sided contributions of the late Dr Figgis.[16]

The ideas of Figgis were to some extent put into practice by William Temple and the *Life and Liberty Movement*, the chief demand of which was 'more self-government for the church; it was to a considerable degree due to the agitation of such men as Temple and Sheppard in this movement that the *Enabling Act* of 1919 was passed, allowing the Church Assembly to present to Parliament legislation on church affairs which must either be accepted or rejected *in toto*, no amendments being allowed. In 1921 the *Scottish Church Act* used

language which is reminiscent of that which Figgis had used
in this context. In particular, article five spoke of the 'inherent right' of church to live its own life, free from state
interference. In England the Church Assembly made use of
its powers in presenting to Parliament a revised Prayer Book
in 1927, which was rejected by the latter body; a further
effort was made in 1928 with a slightly different book, but
this too was turned down. The action of Parliament led to
renewed demands for disestablishment and freedom for the
church. Bishop Charles Gore pleaded that Figgis's theory of
the place of groups in society should be accepted by the
1935 Commission on church and state. The state has, argued
Gore, been disloyal to the church; in the army, in prisons and
in schools the established church is treated as just another
religious group. 'We are,' he pointed out, 'finding ourselves
disestablished almost everywhere except in the lunatic asy-
lums'.[17] The Commission decided not to recommend disestablishment, but an increased freedom within the establishment, though the details need not detain us here. Later
commissions on church and state have recommended more
independence for the church in such matters as the appoint-
ment of bishops, and the control of liturgy and doctrinal
formularies. The most recent commission is clearly divided
on some of the most important theoretical issues at stake;
one section of the commission stated categorically that 'the
State is a secular state', and that bishops of the Church of
England should no longer be selected by the Queen on the
advice of the Prime Minister.[18]

II

There is an obvious relationship between pluralist political
theories on the one hand and movements like syndicalism
and guild socialism on the other. Figgis specifically mentioned the fact that these movements can be seen as possible
consequences of the theories advocated by Maitland and
himself. Laski, Cole and Russell saw a clear link between
their political theories and the guild socialist movement. The
anarcho-syndicalists advocated the abolition of the political
state believing that social life could proceed under the direc-

tion of producer co-operatives, trade guilds and other voluntary associations. The guild socialist modified syndicalist
ideas to allow a place for the state, either as co-ordinator and
controller of the groups, or as the representative of the
consumer.[19] There was in the British labour movement a
prolonged struggle between modified versions of syndicalism
and what *Punch* called 'sydneywebbicalism', or collectivist
state socialism. It was the latter doctrine which carried the
day in the Fabian Society, in the trade union movement and
in the Labour Party. Nevertheless small groups within the
labour movement have continued to reject nationalisation as
the ultimate answer to industrial problems, and have advocated various forms of worker control as the only satisfactory
basis for a socialist society. In recent years there has been a
revival of this tendency in the labour movement associated
with the resurgence of anarchist theories.[20]

Another doctrine which employed the concept of groups
and the challenge to state sovereignty made by Figgis and the
pluralists, was distributivism. This was a variation on the
guild socialist theme. Accepting the notion of the guild
organisation of production, it insisted on a diffusion of the
ownership of property in general and of guild property in
particular, which the guild socialists were not always willing
to allow. Distributivism was an attempt to restore the system
which its supporters believed to have existed in the middle
ages, when the ownership of property was spread out among
the members of the community. To be free, a citizen must
own property, and the associative or distributivist state
would maintain such a situation in being. They attacked the
party system, and advocated·a form of functional representation.[21]

We may briefly allude to a few later developments in the
application of group theories to practical politics. The constitution established by Gabriel d'Annunzio of Fiume included provision for corporations based on function, while the
second chamber, the Council of Provvisori, was functionally
based. Mussolini and the fascists followed d'Annunzio in
some respects, forming a functional assembly and also maintaining a system of syndicates and corporations. Sir Ernest
Barker suggested that the corporative state of fascism was an

attempt to put into practice the Althusian-Gierkian conception of the state as a *communitas communitatum*. Many of
the guild socialists and their sympathisers, such as A. J.
Penty, Ezra Pound, Odon Por and Ramiro de Maeztu became
followers, to a greater or lesser extent, of fascism; they saw in
fascism a theoretical similarity to their own ideas. Others,
however, were not misled by the theory and saw the hard
features of totalitarian autocracy through all the smoke of
corporative propaganda. Lip service to corporativism was also
paid by Nazi Germany.

Another social arrangement which sometimes rests upon
pluralist theories is functionalism, which seeks to replace or
supplement geographical representation by functional representation. It was advocated, as we have already seen, by the
guild socialists and was put into practice in Fascist Italy, in
Weimar Germany and in the post-war West German state of
Bavaria, among other places. In post-war France the M.R.P.
was eager for a functional assembly, but this was opposed by
the socialists, and they had to be content with an Economic
Council. In England there have been various suggestions in
this direction from thinkers as diverse as the guild socialists,
Winston Churchill and Leo Amery. Criticisms have come
from several quarters. Yet there is no necessary connection
between pluralism and functionalism; it is quite possible to
imagine a state which is centralised and functional. A further
institutional implication of political pluralism might be mentioned: this is the proliferation of interest groups of various
kinds in the modern state, and a growing acceptance of these
groups as a legitimate feature of liberal politics. In the final
chapter I shall consider in a little more detail the ideology of
pressure group liberalism which is put forward by a number
of contemporary American political scientists. Here I wish
only to draw attention to the phenomenon of interest
groups. 'Pressure groups', it has been said,

> give us today a genuinely pluralist society in all spheres
> and levels of government. And without pluralism we
> should indeed be helpless before the Great Leviathan.[22]

8 Conclusion

In conclusion I wish to look at the relationship between the political pluralism of Figgis and his contemporaries, and a number of other notions of pluralism.

William James used the term 'pluralism' to describe his own philosophical position, distinguishing it from the monism of contemporary idealist philosophers. While the monist philosophers insisted that the universe is a single, inter-related and coherent totality, which can be known properly only in its totality, 'radical empiricism and pluralism stand out', he claimed,

> for the legitimacy of the notion of *some*: each part of the world is in some ways connected, in some other ways not connected with its other parts, and the ways can be discriminated.[1]

The world of the pluralist, he asserted, is more like a federal republic than an empire or a kingdom,[2] there is always some self-governed aspect remaining, which cannot be reduced to unity. It is likely that a monist in philosophy would reject political pluralism and would hope that the unity which is characteristic of the whole universe might become concrete in institutional form. Nevertheless, as we have seen, a writer like Hegel has certain definite pluralist elements in his understanding of the state as, indeed, did Aristotle. It is not necessarily the case, either, that a philosophical pluralist must be a political pluralist. Yet Figgis and Laski referred occasionally to the pragmatism of James and to the intuitionalism of Bergson in support of their political theories. Philosophical pluralism certainly rules out particular kinds of political monism. The emphasis upon *action* which one finds in James, Bergson and Eucken was drawn upon by Georges Sorel and other syndicalist theorists to support their political doctrines;

Sorel even referred approvingly, on a number of occasions, to the activism of Cardinal Newman. One writer blamed Bergson for encouraging blind irrational action, which is 'precisely what syndicalism needs, to justify its policy'.[3]

In an earlier chapter I have discussed briefly the ethical pluralism of writers like Lippmann and Lamprecht. There I concluded that there is little in common between political and ethical pluralism, and furthermore that most of the English pluralists with whom we are concerned in this monograph would have rejected ethical pluralism.

The term 'pluralism' has increasingly been used in the last few decades by many American political scientists to characterise the system of government which is said to operate in the United States. The notion of pluralism can have both a descriptive and a normative content. Some theorists argue that:

(a) pluralism, as they understand it, is the best form of government, and that

(b) it is more or less realised in the U.S.A.

Others accept pluralism as an ideal, but deny that it is realised in contemporary America. Others again believe that some kind of pluralism does operate in the United States, but deny that it is good. Presumably, to complete the analysis, there are those who neither believe that pluralism is practised nor believe that it ought to be.

Political writers like David Truman write with a certain smugness about the American political system. The most satisfactory system of government is assumed to be a pluralist one, where representative democracy is supplemented by a large number of interest groups, each organised to achieve some specific end, and each endeavouring to influence 'the decision-making process' in accordance with this end. Thus minorities who feel strongly on a particular issue are able to make their voices heard and to influence the course of events. Pluralism is also believed to ensure that power is dispersed throughout the community; there is no single group of people able to determine governmental policy. In the tension which is created by conflicting group interests, individual freedom is thought to be preserved. There is no over-all, total 'common good' or 'public interest', which the government attempts to impose upon the population; it tries simply to reach some temporary compromise between conflicting interests. Government is seen by certain of these writers as an *arena* in which contending groups meet and where some kind of compromise is reached; it is seen by others as the *referee* who searches for some kind of acceptable settlement of the conflicting claims made by groups. Clearly, the latter view is, in some respects, similar to that which Figgis advocated.

Many American pluralist writers believe that pluralism is the best form of government, and also that it is the form of government which operates in the United States. It is the pattern which 'modernising' nations must ever keep before their eyes. There is no system of government in all of history, declared Nelson D. Rockefeller after his celebrated tour of Latin America, 'better than our own flexible structure of political democracy, individual initiative, and responsible citizenship in elevating the quality of man's life'.[4]

In *The Torment of Secrecy*, Edward Shils puts forward a pluralist theory (as he conceives of it). He clearly believes that a pluralist society is not only the best kind of society, but is also the basic form of society which exists in the United States. The McCarthyism of the early fifties is seen by him to be an aberration, a deviation from the American way of life, a disease temporarily afflicting an otherwise healthy body politic. This pluralism involves tolerating a large number of groups, so long as their demands are 'moderate'; that is, so long as their members do not go to 'an extreme in zealous attachment to a particular value'.[5] If a group is content to demand a little more of what it thinks good, rather than the complete fulfilment of its dreams, it can 'fall within the circle of pluralism'. He sees this pluralist society as one composed of 'leaders and led', in which there must be 'a sense of affinity among the elites'.[6] This sense of affinity involves not an agreement to live and let live, but a determination to seek some kind of common good which will be imposed by the state, and which will reflect as far as possible the common interests of these acceptable in-groups; it also clearly implies the suppression of those groups which are thought to be 'extreme', whose leaders (presuming they are composed of leaders and led) do not feel a sense of affinity with the leaders of other groups, or who reject the idea that a state should be concerned with imposing upon the population a substantive purpose, even though this purpose is thought to be the result of a general consensus among the majority. Shils sees in the United States a situation where there is a general agreement among right-thinking people, those whom President Nixon refers to as the 'silent majority', those who feel strongly about nothing except the preservation of a state in which no one is permitted to feel strongly about anything else. In the United States, businessmen may be called upon by the administration for certain tasks, but 'when they serve, they do not do so as businessmen but as government officials'.[7] In fact, one such businessman has gone further, and asserted that there is no distinction between the two roles.

This double claim that pluralism is American and that it is good has led unfriendly critics to declare that pluralism is little more than an ideology (in the prejorative sense); that it is simply being used as the intellectual justification for perpetuating a *status quo* which is really defended on quite other grounds. Perhaps the most celebrated attack upon these American pluralist theories came from C. Wright Mills in his book on *The Power Elite*, where he argued forcefully that American society was controlled by a coherent and sinister elite group, which determined all the important decisions of government according to their own narrow interests. This view gained a certain kind of popularity when President Eisenhower referred to a 'military-industrial complex' in the course of his farewell address.[8]

Pluralist writers have replied to the Mills theory of a power elite by making the general criticism that his theory is much too impressionistic, vague and lacking in empirical support. Also they have conducted a number of empirical studies of power distribution in the United States, concentrating particularly on the local and regional levels of government. Robert Dahl's study of power in the city of New Haven, *Who*

Governs?, is a classic in this field. His aim is to show that there are a number of quite distinct groups which have an effective voice in key decisions made in the city. Dahl's critics point out, however, that in over-emphasising the actual process of decision-making, he ignores all those forces which are able to prevent an issue from coming to the fore at all. Also it is observed that there is no clear criterion suggested for determining which issues are the 'key issues'. Nevertheless, these faults in Dahl's method do nothing to rehabilitate the assertions of Mills with respect to the existence of a power elite. Even radical critics of American life, like R. P. Wolff, are dissatisfied with the 'power elite' theory. But the more valid point made by Mills was that the interest group system, as it operates in the United State, militates against large sections of the American public — the poor, the blacks and, in general, the unorganised. This fact has recently been reiterated by Wolff, who insists that the contemporary American state is organised in such a way that the well-established groups have their interests taken into account, but emerging groups find it difficult to make their voices heard. There is in America a great deal of intolerance of marginal, unrespectable groups who refuse to subscribe to the generally accepted norms of the average citizen. H. Marcuse has argued in a similar vein. Most of these criticisms are directed against pluralism as a descriptive theory, rather than against its normative aspect. What these writers are saying up to this point is that contemporary American society is not, in fact, a genuine pluralist society.

Some critics go further and attack the pluralist ideal; or, at least, they attack certain corollaries of pluralism. H. S. Kariel has argued that the organisations which in the past were, with some justification, thought of as protecting the individual against unjust claims by the government, have themselves become oligarchic and oppressive. 'Our problem today', he writes,

> . . . is not how to strengthen the hierarchies of organized private power, but rather how to control them by some means short of establishing an illiberal political order.[9]

In recent years there has been a revival of Rousseau's idea of

a general will. Wolff attempts to show that the notion of a
common good is meaningful, and is a possible object of state
policy. 'There must be some way,' he maintains, 'of constituting the whole society a genuine group with a group purpose and a conception of the common good'.[10] He correctly
perceives that most versions of pluralism would rule out such
a project as impossible. Furthermore, most pluralists would
insist that any attempt to constitute a society of the kind
envisaged by Wolff, having some single, coherent, all-
embracing substantive purpose, would necessarily end in
totalitarianism.

The difference between the European and the American
conceptions of a pluralist state is not so much that the
former is characterised by 'order', while in the latter we find
'a kaleidoscopic array of special interests'[11] — that one is
static and the other is dynamic — the difference is rather that
American pluralist theories see the group as exerting an
influence in order to persuade the government to perform
some substantive good which will be in the interest of that
group. The really significant difference is that most American
theories see the groups as 'feverishly seeking to penetrate the
policy-making arena',[12] or competing 'for control over the
actions of the government'.[13] These theories assume that the
government will, and ought to, play an active and substantive
role in determining the course of events. They see the various
groups bringing pressure to bear on the government, pulling it
hither and yon, in an effort to persuade it to bestow its
patronage in such a way as to benefit their own particular
interests. From what has been said in previous chapters, it
will be clear that, between these contemporary American
theories and the notion of pluralism advocated by Figgis,
there is a great gulf fixed. The English pluralists believed that
the associations which comprise the state should not endeavour to force the government actively to intervene in the
life of the people in order to realise some substantive purpose. These associations should be concerned simply with
obtaining freedom to live life in a manner which they prefer,
while recognising the rights of other groups to a similar
freedom. If groups and parties in the state spent as much
energy and money pursuing concrete ends of their choice, as

they now spend on trying to persuade governments to pursue these ends on their behalf, the world would be a better place. The history of the labour movement in Britain provides an awful example of pressure group politics. Every five years or so, extraordinary efforts are made to put into political office a party which is believed to be in sympathy with the movement, and a number of other stratagems are employed in order to get Parliament to do what the movement might well have done on its own. The industrial scene might have been very much brighter than it is today if workers had concentrated upon direct action along the lines recommended by the guild socialists, and tried to ensure that the state played as small a role as possible in the industrial affairs of the nation.

Recent theories of social and cultural pluralism must clearly be distinguished from the political pluralism with which this monograph is concerned. J. S. Furnivall employed the term 'plural society' to describe a type of society which resulted from the European colonisation of tropical lands. A plural society, according to Furnivall, exists when there are a number of distinct groups living side by side, but separately; they meet only in the market-place. Religious, cultural, racial and linguistic divisions reinforce one another so that the groups form quite distinct blocks. The political entity is held together, not by shared values or by common institutions, but by force, which is exercised by an elite of colonial administrators and their local collaborators who form a small but coherent minority in the society. Furnivall also claimed that these groups into which plural societies are divided are not natural, organic associations, but are aggregates of individuals — they are crowds and not communities. The capitalist economic system which has been the invariable companion of imperial expansion led to the break-up of village life and of traditional ties.[14] These ideas have been modified and developed by M. G. Smith, L. Kuper, P. L. van den Berghe and others, who apply the concept of social and cultural pluralism to the post-colonial nations of Africa and the Caribbean.[15] Curiously, Ralph Dahrendorf uses the term 'pluralism' in a completely opposite sense, and differentiates pluralism from what he calls superimposition, as ideal types of society. In a society of the latter type all divisions among the population reinforce one another:

> political class conflict, industrial class conflict, regional conflicts, conflicts between town and country, possibly racial and religious conflicts all are superimposed so as to form a single and all-embracing antagonism.[16]

In what he calls pluralist society conflicts are dissociated, exclusion from the dominant or majority group in one sphere does not necessarily imply exclusion in other spheres; there is what another sociologist called a *web* of group affiliations.[17] Thus a plural society, as understood by Furnival and Smith, is practically equivalent to Dahrendorf's superimposed society, and is therefore opposed to his notion of a pluralist society.

How does the political pluralism of Figgis and his contemporaries relate to the social and cultural pluralism of Furnivall (or to the superimposed society of Dahrendorf)? When the English pluralists talked about groups in a state, they more or less assumed that most men would belong to a number of different groups which were not coterminous in their membership. Roman Catholics, protestants and atheists might well be fellow members of a trade union or a local cricket club. They were looking principally at the situation in Britain, which is a relatively non-segmented country, rather than at plural societies (in Furnivall's sense). Their theory was essentially normative (though, as we have seen in chapter 4, it was to some extent based upon their assessment of social facts), while the theory of Furnivall and Smith is purely descriptive. Nevertheless it would be possible to apply the theory of political pluralism to those nations where group divisions are superimposed. The likelihood of serious and violent conflict occurring in such situations is greater than it is in states where group affiliations overlap. It might at first appear to be wise, in countries where divisions are superimposed, for the government to adopt a dynamic policy of national integration, using all the means in its power to inculcate a national culture and impose a uniform system of values upon the population. According to this view, the political pluralism of Figgis could safely be pursued only in relatively homogeneous states or where conflicts are dissociated; political pluralism would be disastrous in Furnivall's plural societies. This argument appears to be one which is accepted, implicitly or explicitly, by a large number of the leaders of the new nations, who are egged on by an almost endless procession of 'nation-building' political scientists, and 'missions' composed of international 'experts' of unbelievable dreariness and overweening self-confidence. At least, the older type of missionary stayed for more than five weeks in a country before thinking that he could prescribe a solution to national problems.

Now this is a false view of the situation, as some governments are beginning to discover. The very attempt, made by a government, to achieve national unity is often seen by minority groups as constituting a threat to their existence or to their way of life. Thus by following a dynamic policy of national unification, a state may well bring upon itself that very disintegration which it was the purpose of the policy to avoid. The government will in any case find the task of maintaining order a difficult one; eventually the state may split into two or more parts. In some circumstances there may be no way of avoiding this. But so far as distinct associations and multiple loyalties exist within a single political entity, it behoves the government to recognise their existence and allow these groups as much freedom to arrange their own affairs as is compatible with peace and order. Furthermore, as Hegel reminded his contemporaries, governments are often weakened by attempting to achieve too much, and by becoming involved in unnecessary enterprises. If a government becomes involved in activities other than those concerned with maintaining order and defending the state against external attack, thus demanding from the citizen obedience in these additional matters, the citizens are likely to confuse the necessary tasks of the government with these extra functions, 'become as impatient with the one as with the other, and bring the state, as regards its necessary claims, into jeopardy'.[18]

Trinidad is sometimes referred to by anthropologists as a country which manifests a high level of social and cultural pluralism, and which therefore approaches the ideal type of a plural society, but there is a considerable degree of overlap in group affiliations. Indian businessmen join with French Creoles, Syrians and Chinese in chambers of commerce; Portuguese, Chinese and Negroes are fellow Roman Catholics; there are rich Hindus and poor Hindus; urban Muslims may join one political party while their rural co-religionists may support a rival party. No doubt, racial loyalties are often stronger than any others, though the recent black power movement would seem to indicate that divisions among Negro Trinidadians can at times be as significant as divisions along racial lines.[19] The pluralist theories of Figgis and his contemporaries could certainly apply to a country like Trinidad. Racial, religious, cultural and economic groups must be recognised by the state and should be left to pursue those ends which they set for themselves, within a framework of order. Pluralists would encourage the groups themselves to be more active and creative, and not to spend all their energy persuading the government to do those things which they could perfectly well do for themselves. Perhaps one of the most significant developments in recent years has been the take-over by a trade union of a number of restaurants. If the men who actually work in the establishments will really have an effective voice in determining how they are run, progress will have been made. The danger is, of course, that the restaurants will be controlled by a trade union bureaucracy in Port of Spain, and not by the workers involved. Cultural associations like the Chinese Association, the Himalaya Club and the Portuguese Association could play a much more constructive role in the country than they do. Why, until recently, has there been little support for forming an African Association? These cultural groups should not be regarded with suspicion by the state, nor should their exclusivism necessarily be condemned. Any rigorous efforts by the government to impose upon the population a single 'creole' culture will be interpreted by minority groups as an attack upon their interests.

The idea that a state can exist only when the people share a common set of values is mistaken. Even in a relatively homogeneous state like the United Kingdom, values differ quite radically from one section of the population to another. Certainly, a majority of the people must share a belief in the importance of civil peace, combined with a willingness to allow their fellow citizens to live life as they choose to live it. They must also recognise some machinery which is the normal channel for resolving disputes — though this recognition will never be absolute. Individuals and groups will retain the ultimate right to use force in defending those rights which they believe to be vital. But the idea that governments must play an active and dynamic role in imposing or inculcating a single culture or set of values will lead either to totalitarianism or to civil war. 'The more conscience comes to the front,' wrote Acton, 'the more we consider, not what the state accomplishes, but what it allows to be accomplished'.[20]

Notes

The following abbreviations are used in the notes:

Authority: H. J. Laski, *Authority in the Modern State.*
Chaos: G. D. H. Cole, *Chaos and Order in Industry.*
Churches: J. N. Figgis, *Churches in the Modern State.*
Divine Right: J. N. Figgis, *The Divine Right of Kings.*
Essays: Lord Acton, *Essays on Freedom and Power.*
Fellowship: J. N. Figgis, *The Fellowship of the Mystery.*
Genossenschaftstheorie: O. von Gierke, *Die Genossenschaftstheorie und die deutsche Rechtsprechung.*
Gerson: J. N. Figgis, *Studies of Political Thought from Gerson to Grotius 1414-1625.*
Grammar: H. J. Laski, *A Grammar of Politics.*
'Grundbegriffe': O. von Gierke, 'Die Grundbegriffe des Staatsrechts' in *30 Zeitschrift für die gesammte Staatswissenschaft* (1874).
Hopes: J. N. Figgis, *Hopes for English Religion.*
Labour: G. D. H. Cole, *Labour in the Commonwealth.*
Political Theories: O. von Gierke, *Political Theories of the Middle Age* (edited with an introduction by F. W. Maitland).
Problem: H. J. Laski, *Studies in the Problem of Sovereignty.*
Self-Government: G. D. H. Cole, *Self-Government in Industry.*
Wesen: O. von Gierke, *Das Wesen der menschlichen Verbände.*

1 INTRODUCTION: PARENTALISM AND PLURALISM

1. I do not wish to suggest that ideologies are merely rationalisations of self-interested groups or classes (though the word is frequently used in this pejorative sense). I hope to deal in more detail elsewhere with this topic. Here I would merely assert (a) that it is impossible to understand human actions fully unless we see them as purposive, and often following from conscious decisions or choices; (b) that the choices and decisions which a person makes are closely related to the beliefs which he holds; (c) that these beliefs cannot satisfactorily be accounted for simply as mechanical consequences of physiological or social conditions; (d) that a person sometimes holds beliefs because he thinks them to be true, and that one way of changing these beliefs is to convince him that they are false; and (e) that it is often important to consider whether a belief is true or not, and that this inquiry is distinct from (though sometimes connected to) a discussion about the origin of the belief.

2. I have considered in another place the way in which liberalism was transformed into a theory of positive state action at the turn of the century. Cf. David Nicholls, 'Positive Liberty 1880-1914', in 56 *American Political Science Review* (1962).
3. In W. E. Connolly (ed.), *The Bias of Pluralism*, p. 95. This is a useful collection of critical essays on contemporary American pluralism.
4. *Evolutioñary Socialism*, p. 169.
5. In G. B. Shaw (ed.), *Fabian Essays*, p. 182.
6. In ibid., p. 60. In some of his later writings, however, Webb was not quite so optimistic about the outcome of this glide; cf. *Towards Social Democracy*.
7. Margaret Cole, *The Story of Fabian Socialism*, p. 148.
8. *Political Parties*, p. 113.
9. It is the fundamental right of every human being 'to be protected from his own weaknesses' (Senator R. Neehall of Trinidad; *Trinidad Hansard:* Senate Debates, 27 Nov 1968).
10. *Churches*, p. 57.
11. 7 *The Independent Review* (1905) p. 19.
12. J. F. Stephen, *Liberty Equality Fraternity*, p. 256; cf. also H. Maine, *Popular Government*, p.32; on Balfour cf. David Nicholls, 'Few are Chosen', *30 The Review of Politics* (1968) pp. 33f.
13. *Churches*, p. 150.
14. Ibid., p. 135.
15. Cf. infra chapter 6.
16. *Notes towards the Definition of Culture*, p. 60.
17. *Politics*, 5:11.
18. *L'idée générale de la révolution au 19e siècle*, p. 344.
19. For earlier discussions of English political pluralism see K. C. Hsiao, *Political Pluralism;* H. M. Magid, *English Political Pluralism;* W. Y. Elliott, *The Pragmatic Revolt in Politics;* F. W. Coker, 'The Technique of the Pluralistic State', *15 American Political Science Review* (1921) pp. 186f; E. D. Ellis, 'Guild Socialism and Pluralism', *17 American Political Science Review* (1923) pp. 584f; E. D. Ellis 'The Pluralist State', *14 American Political Science Review*, pp. 393f; N. Wilde, 'The Attack on the State' *30 International Journal of Ethics* (1900) pp. 349f; G. Sabine, 'Pluralism: a point of view', *17 American Political Science Review* (1923) pp. 34f; L. Rockow *Contemporary Political Thought in England*, chapters 6 and 7; other literature will be mentioned in the text and in the bibliography.

2 LIBERTY AND THE DIVISION OF POWER

1. *In Defence of Politics*, p. 21.
2. *A Preface to Morals*, pp. 112-3.
3. 'A person is composed of an internalization of organized social roles.' H. H. Gerth and C. Wright Mills, *Character and Social Structure*, p. 83; cf. also J. H. Fichter, *Sociology*, p. 212, and T. M. Newcomb, 'Community Roles in Attitude Formation', in 7 *American Sociological Review* (1942) pp. 621f.
4. 'The Need for a Pluralistic Emphasis in Ethics', in *17 Journal of Philosophy Psychology and Scientific Method* (1920) pp. 562, 569.

5. *Methods of Ethics*, pp. 106-7; the same elementary point is made by popular moral philosophers of our own day, cf. R. M. Hare, *The Language of Morals*, pp. 151f, and P. H. Nowell-Smith, *Ethics*, pp. 185f.

6. 'The Metaphysical Basis of Toleration', in *Works*, vi 227.

7. *The Process of Government*, p. 371; cf. also T. V. Smith, *The Legislative Way of Life* and *The Compromise Principle in Politics.*

8. *Churches*, p. 263.

9. *Authority*, p. 121.

10. Op. cit. p. 128. In his *Four Essays on Liberty* Sir Isaiah Berlin implies that Bentham saw that 'some laws increase the total amount of liberty in a society' (p. xlix). I am not convinced that he did. Bentham certainly 'favoured laws', but he justified them in só far as they increased happiness or diminished pain, rather than in terms of increasing the total amount of liberty. This is what would distinguish him from a writer like Hobhouse, who insisted that laws can increase the total freedom in society (though, of course, they diminish the freedom of those persons who are coerced). Hobhouse thus put forward an explicitly *liberal* defence of legislation, which Bentham did not do. See also David Nicholls 'Positive Liberty 1880-1914', *56 American Political Science Review* (1962) pp. 114f.

11. *The Metaphysical Theory of the State*, p. 36.

12. Op. cit., p. 128.

13. *Principles of Political Economy*, book 5, chap. 11.

14. 'The State in Recent Political Theory', *Political Quarterly*, Feb 1914 p. 128.

15. *Churches*, p. 116.

16. *Authority*, pp. 54-5.

17. *On Liberty*, chap. 1. Cf. also 'I fully admit that the mischief which a person does to himself may seriously affect, both through their sympathies and their interests, those nearly connected with him and, in a minor degree, society at large. . . .' Ibid., chap. 4.

18. *The History of Freedom*, p. 203.

19. Cambridge University Library, Add. MSS. 4901:20.

20. *Life and Letters of Mandell Creighton*, i 263.

21. 'The Literature of Politics', *13 New Republic*, 17 Nov 1917, p. 6.

22. *Letter to the Duke of Norfolk*, p. 53.

23. *Hopes*, p. 116.

24. *From Pluralism to Collectivism*, p. 38.

25. *The Rambler*, Jan 1860, p. 146.

26. *The History of Freedom*, p. 3.

27. *Hopes*, p. 114.

28. *Authority*, p. 55. Green wrote of freedom as 'a positive power of doing or enjoying something worth doing or enjoying, and that, too, something that we do or enjoy in common with others'. *Works*, iii 371.

29. *Authority*, p. 37.

30. *Grammar*, p. 142. In later editions Laski changed this passage.

31. *Social Theory*, p. 184.

32. Ibid., p. 182.

33. *Labour*, p. 194.

34. *Self-Government,* p. 227.
35. *Principles of Social Reconstruction,* p. 228.
36. *Political Ideals,* p. 10.
37. *Journeys to England,* p. 24.
38. Quoted in J. Charles-Brun's introduction to Proudhon's *Principe fédératif,* p. 123n.
39. Mirfield MSS.
40. Lecture on Aquinas, Mirfield MSS., notebook 2.
41. *Essays,* p. 35.
42. Lecture III on Marsilius; Mirfield MSS., notebook 3.
43. *Essays,* p. 101.
44. H. R. Niebuhr, *The Kingdom of God in America,* pp. 77f.
45. *Essays,* p. 48.
46. Ibid., p. 63.
47. *Letters to Mary Gladstone,* p. 124.
48. Introduction to Gierke, *Political Theories,* p. xliii.
49. G. P. Gooch in foreword to G. Ritter, *The Corrupting Influence of Power,* p. x.
50. *Authority,* p. 387.
51. Ibid., p. 90.
52. *Réflexions sur la violence,* p. 151.
53. *Political Ideals,* pp. 11-12 and *Principles of Social Reconstruction,* p. 73. Cf. the attitude of one of the critics of pluralism: 'it is not force that is dangerous but the will embodied in it. The problem, therefore, is not that of limiting sovereignty, but of educating the sovereign.' Norman Wilde 'The Attack on the State', *30 International Journal of Ethics* (1920) p. 370.
54. 'Substance of the speech on the army estimates' 1790 in *Works,* III 9-10.
55. Georges Goyau, *Ketteler,* p. 41. This association idea was, he held, particularly strong with the German people, *Die Arbeiterfrage und das Christenthum,* pp. 49-50. Gierke continually made the same point in *Das deutsche Genossenschaftsrecht;* cf. ii 32.
56. 'This pulverisation method, this chemical solution of humanity into individuals, into grains of dust equal in value, into particles which a puff of the wind may scatter in all directions — this method is as false as are the suppositions on which it rests.' *Die Arbeiterfrage,* p. 57. Cf. J. F. Stephen's remark, 'The existence of such a state of society reduces individuals to impotence, and to tell them to be powerful, original and independent is to mock them. It is like plucking a bird's feathers in order to put it on a level with beasts, and then telling it to fly.' *Liberty Equality Fraternity,* p. 46.
57. 'Moral Personality and Legal Personality' in *Collected Papers,* iii 311. Infra, p. 162.
58. *Antichrist,* p. 266.
59. *Churches,* p. 101.
60. S. Mogi, *The Problem of Federalism,* p. 312.
61. *Churches,* p. 81.
62. Figgis in A. J. Mason *et al., Our Place in Christendom,* p. 94.
63. *Essays,* p. 160.
64. *Churches,* p. 101.

65. Ibid., p. 101. Cf. H. Butterfield, *The Historical Development of the Principle of Toleration in British Life*, p. 3.
66. W. K. Jordan, *The Development of Religious Toleration in England*, i 19. For a discussion of the growth of toleration in the U.S.A. cf. A. P. Stokes *Church and State in the United States*, especially i 244.
67. 'A Puritan Utopia', *Church Quarterly Review* (1903) p. 126.
68. For example, A. A. Seaton, *The Theory of Toleration under the Later Stuarts*, p. 18. Maitland seems to have held this view too: 'Scepticism or doubt is the legitimate parent of toleration.' 'Liberty and Equality' (1875) in *Collected Papers* i 95.
69. *Gerson*, p. 118.
70. *Churches*, p. 101.
71. *Holmes-Laski Letters*, pp. 246-7.
72. *Gerson*, p. 180.

3   THE ATTACK ON SOVEREIGNTY

1. *Studies in History and Jurisprudence*, ii 50.
2. *The Province of Jurisprudence Determined*, pp. 225 and 244.
3. *Lectures on the Early History of Institutions*, pp. 358-9.
4. *Introduction to the Study of the Law of the Constitution*, pp. 70-1. F. W. Coker, however, criticising the ideas of Laski, denied that 'any political philosopher of any school in any era' has maintained this notion of a practical sovereign having unlimited power. 'The Technique of the Pluralistic State', *15 American Political Science Review* (1921) p. 194.
5. *Principles of State Interference*, p. 68. Cf. also *Darwin and Hegel*, pp. 238f. Ritchie maintained that in the U.S.A. the constitution was sovereign.
6. Op. cit., ii 63.
7. Ibid., ii 73.
8. Cf. also W. Y. Elliott, who wrote of '... that intangible but sovereign thing called public opinion.' *The Pragmatic Revolt in Politics*, p. 272.
9. That is, he might say that it *must* have been the will of the electors, or it would not have prevailed.
10. *The Elements of Politics*, p. 658.
11. *Mind*, Oct 1950, pp. 495f. It is reprinted in W. J. Stankiewicz (ed.), in *Defence of Sovereignty*, pp. 209f. Stankiewicz himself apparently attempts to defend the use of 'the classical concept' of sovereignty. His whole essay is, however, a monument of confusion, and it is quite impossible to make sense of what he writes. Perhaps this is due to a defect in his understanding of the English language. Ibid., pp. 3f.
12. *Leviathan*, 2:21.
13. *Groundwork of the Metaphysic of Morals*, chap. 2.
14. Op. cit., p. 8.
15. Ibid., p. 26.
16. *Genossenschaftstheorie*, pp. 641-2. Gierke's pupil Hugo Preuss criticised him on this question of sovereignty, maintaining that the theory of group personality maintained by Gierke logically

implies a rejection of the traditional ideas about state sovereignty. *Gemeinde, Staat, Reich*, p. 112.

17. Expounding the ideas of Althusius, Gierke wrote, 'Moreover it [the state] is not absolute but bound by legal limitations, even though it may seem exempt from positive law so far as compulsion and punishment are concerned.' *The Development of Political Theory*, p. 40; cf. also Gierke's discussion of the ideas of Althusius in *Natural Law and the Theory of Society*, pp. 70f.

18. Introduction to *Natural Law and the Theory of Society*, p. 1xxxii.

19. That is in a sociological sense at least. 'I must emphasise', writes S. Mogi, 'the fact that the aims and methods of Gierke's *Genossenschaftstheorie* are pluralistic in essence . . . and not unitarist'. *Otto von Gierke*, p. 230. But cf. Mogi's earlier view: 'Gierke's theory stands midway between the pluralistic and unitaristic tendencies. Therefore the interpretation put upon his theory of the state differs largely according to the standpoint of his critics, i.e. whether they themselves are unitarists or pluralists. But the main maxim of the *Genossenschaftstheorie* is based on "unity in plurality", i.e. pluralistic in principle.' *The Problem of Federalism*, p. 1084n.

20. *Gerson*, p. 171.

21. 'For my part, I am of opinion that this marriage, which before was contrary to the Law of God merely because the statute condemned it as such, is so no longer, and that by virtue of the statute which legalises it.' Quoted in *Churches*, p. 5n.

22. Lecture III on Marsilius, Mirfield MSS, Notebook 3. Cf. the words of Acton: 'According to the old conservative legitimist principles the right of authority ought always to be sustained in case of revolution — and the new democratic doctrine is that the will of the people ought ever to prevail. . . . Both personify right. They talk of the rights of government or of the people. But the supreme right is the divine right; and that is to be found sometimes on the one side and sometimes on the other. There is no general presumption either way.' From a document in the possession of Mr Douglas Woodruff, who kindly let me look at some of the Acton MSS which he has.

23. That is the notion of sovereignty.

24. Lecture on Aquinas, Mirfield MSS Notebook 2.

25. 'Conflicting Social Obligations', in *15 Proceedings of the Aristotelian Society* (1914-15) p. 152; cf. also *Self-Government*, p. 82. Cole's position is basically that of Rousseau, and Bosanquet congratulated him on this. 'Note on Mr Cole's Paper', *15 Proceedings of the Aristotelian Society* (1914-15) p. 161.

26. Cole, 'Conflicting Social Obligations', p. 157. It has been said that Cole later abandoned his Rousseauism in an unfinished book on Rousseau (N. Carpenter, *Guild Socialism*, p. 89n.). Cole certainly rejected the ideas of S. G. Hobson on sovereignty; cf. Hobson, *National Guilds and the State*, pp. 107, 122, 127.

27. *Political Thought in England*, p. 223. Yet Barker later denied ever having held a pluralist doctrine which, 'dissolves and divides the sovereignty of the State among a plurality of different groups or communities'. *Age and Youth*, p. 76.

28.   *La politique*, p. 56.
29.   *Law in the Modern State*, p. 40.
30.   Sub-heading to T. H. Green, *Lectures on the Principles of Political Obligation*, section G.
31.   Laski, 'The Pluralistic State', in *28 The Philosophical Review* (1919) p. 571. Infra., pp. 152-3.
32.   *Problem*, p. 23.
33.   *Reason and Nature*, p. 398 (my italics).
34.   'Compulsion' in J. A. Hobson and M. Ginsberg, *L. T. Hobhouse*, pp. 318-9.
35.   *Grammar*, p. 44. Cole, however, asserted just this; 'There clearly must in the end,' he wrote, 'be somewhere in the society an ultimate court of appeal, whether determinate or not'. Introduction to Rousseau, *The Social Contract*, p. xxvi. What an indeterminate court is like he did not say!
36.   'The State in Recent Political Theory', in *The Political Quarterly'* (1914) pp. 134-5.
37.   'Conflicting Social Obligations', in *15 Proceedings of the Aristotelian Society* (1914-15) p. 158, and *Self-Government*, p. 84.
38.   *Divine Right*, p. 232.
39.   Ibid., p. 246.
40.   'On Some Political Theories of the Early Jesuits', in *Transactions of the Royal Historical Society*, 1897, p. 107.
41.   *Churches*, p. x.
42.   Although there are still some difficulties; for example, is Parliament recognised as sovereign because common law holds it to be sovereign? If so, there is a sense in which common law is superior to statute law. Certain laws are not in any construction commands, but are regulations governing procedures; Austin's theory cannot cover these.
43.   'The Pluralistic State', p. 565. Infra., p. 147.
44.   Jurisprudents, however, are often unwilling to accept the concept of legal sovereignty as necessary to a satisfactory theory of law. Professor Hart has stated that 'the general acceptance of the authority of a lawmaking procedure, irrespective of the changing individuals who operate it from time to time, can be only distorted by an analysis in terms of mass habitual obedience to certain persons who are by definition outside the law'. *71 Harvard Law Review* (1958) p. 604.
45.   *Holmes-Laski Letters*, p. 9n.
46.   *Pollock-Holmes Letters*, ii 25.
47.   'The Law and the State' in *31 Harvard Law Review* (1917) p. 158. Cf. also *L'Etat, le droit objectif et la loi positive*, pp. 131f. Pollock wrote: 'Law is enforced by the State because it is law; it is not law merely because the State enforces it.' *A First Book of Jurisprudence*, p. 29.
48.   W. Jethro Brown, 'The Personality of the Corporation and the State', in *21 Law Quarterly Review* (1905) p. 377.
49.   *Lecture on Aquinas*, Mirfield MSS Notebook 2.

4   GROUP PERSONALITY

1.   *Lectures on the Early History of Institutions*, p. 396.

2. I have discussed the political ideas of these men briefly in 'Positive Liberty, 1880-1914', *American Political Science Review*, March 1962.

3. *The Division of Labor*, p. 28; see also H. E. Barnes, 'Durkheim's Contribution to the Reconstruction of Political Theory', *35 Political Science Quarterly* (1920) pp. 236f. also S. Lukes, *Emile Durkheim: His Life and Work*, pp. 542f.

4. *Ethical Studies*, p. 157.

5. In Gierke, *Political Theories*, p. xli.

6. *Churches*, pp. 87-8.

7. Ibid., p. 48.

8. P. T. Forsyth, *Theology in Church and State*, pp. 160, 206.

9. *Grammar*, p. 256.

10. *Problem*, pp. 208-9.

11. Ibid., p. 4. Cf. also 'The Apotheosis of the State', *7 The New Republic* (July 1916) p. 303.

12. *University of Chicago Law Review*, 15 (1948) p. 580.

13. *Authority*, p. 68. Cf. discussion of this matter in B. Zylstra, op cit., p. 53f.

14. *Labour*, p. 38.

15. *Political Thought in England*, p. 153.

16. 'The Discredited State', *The Political Quarterly* (Feb 1915) p. 113.

17. *Philosophy and Psycho-analysis*, p. 9. Among contemporary British philosophers there are those who are critical of reductionism. Cf. J. O. Urmson, *Philosophical Analysis*, p. 152, and P. F. Strawson, *Individuals*, pp. 110f.

18. *Ideals and Illusions*, pp. 162f.

19. *TVA and the Grass Roots*, p. 258.

20. 'The Combination Laws', in *17 Harvard Law Review* (1904) p. 532.

21. *Systems of Modern Roman Law*, sec. 60 (E.T. of second volume is entitled *Jural Relations*, ii 1-2). Corporate persons are thus 'artificial subjects admitted by means of a pure fiction,' ibid., sec. 85, ii 176.

22. Gierke, *Das deutsche Genossenschaftsrecht*, iii 279; Figgis accepted this view (*Churches*, p. 249). H. A. Smith criticised this view, arguing that Innocent was not concerned with 'the working out of purely speculative theories' (*The Law of Associations*, p. 156). This may be true, but Figgis argued that the Pope's statements on practical questions assumed something very like the fiction theory (*English Historical Review*, 1916, p. 177).

23. Detailed references to cases discussed in the monograph can be found in a table on p. 137.

24. *Essays in the Law*, p. 153.

25. For a more detailed discussion of Gierke's ideas, cf. J. D. Lewis, *The Genossenschaft Theory of Otto von Gierke*.

26. 'Grundbegriffe', p. 302.

27. *Wesen*, p. 10. Cf. also 'Den Kern der Genossenschaftstheorie bildet die von ihr dem Phantom der persona ficta entgegengestellte Auffassung der Körperschaft als *realer Gesammtperson*', *Genossenschaftstheorie*, p. 5.

28. *Sutton's Hospital* Case.

29. *Osborne* Case.
30. *Kent & Sussex Contractors.*
31. *Great Northern Railway* Case.
32. Report of the Committee on Company Law Amendment (1945), Cmd. 6659, p. 9.
33. L. C. B. Gower, *Modern Company Law*, p. 93.
34. *Collected Papers*, iii 319.
35. *Fellowship*, p. 74.
36. M. de Wolfe Howe, 'Political Theory and the Nature of Liberty', 67 *Harvard Law Review* (1953), p. 93.
37. *Our Place in Christendom*, p. 131.
38. *Legal Personality and Political Pluralism*, p. 55.
39. Op. cit., p. 179. It is also clear from ibid., p. 250, that Figgis was fully aware that the effects of the decision were mitigated by legislation.
40. *Essays in the Law*, p. 167.
41. *Grammar*, p. 256 (my italics).
42. *Salmond on Jurisprudence* (11th edition), pp. 362-3.
43. *The Freedom of the Will*, p. 79.
44. 70 *Law Quarterly Review* (1954) p. 56.
45. *The Group Basis of Politics*, p. 8.
46. Op. cit., p. vi.
47. Gierke does, however, seem to suggest on occasions that his belief in the social reality of groups is derived from the fact that they are treated as persons in law. *Wesen*, p. 15.
48. Op. cit., p. 52.
49. *The Law Relating to Unincorporated Associations*, pp. 4-5.
50. In Gierke, *Political Theories*, p. xxxviii.

5   THE STATE, THE GROUP AND THE INDIVIDUAL

1. Op. cit., pp. 574f.
2. The term 'coerce' is widely defined and includes such things as banding together to boycott certain goods (ibid., p. 578). An attempt to prevent this kind of group action would, for example, deprive black people in southern Africa today of the one means short of violence which they have for exercising political influence.
3. Ibid., p. 588.
4. *Philosophy of Right*, paragraphs 302f.
5. T. M. Knox and Z. A. Pelczynski (eds.), *Hegel's Political Writings*, p. 158.
6. *Philosophy of Right*, paragraph 288.
7. 'The Group Basis of Politics', 46 *American Political Science Review* (1952) p. 379.
8. 'Conflicting Social Obligations', 15 *Proceedings of the Aristotelian Society* (1914-15) p. 142.
9. R. M. MacIver, *The Modern State*, p. 170n.
10. *English Political Pluralism*, pp. 26-7.
11. B. Zylstra, op. cit., p. 192.
12. *Churches*, p. 103.

13. 'Erastianism' in Ollard, Cross and Bond (eds.), *Dictionary of English Church History*, p. 211.
14. *Churches*, p. 251.
15. *Divine Right*, p. 292.
16. *Churches*, p. 90, and *Antichrist*, p. 259.
17. Cf. J. Dewey, *Reconstruction in Philosophy*, p. 203.
18. *Churches*, pp. 252-3.
19. Lecture on Aquinas, *Mirfield MSS.* Notebook 2.
20. *Churches*, p. 252.
21. 'The Combination Laws', in *17 Harvard Law Review* (1904) p. 514.
22. *Churches*, p. 46.
23. "The Church and the Secular Theory of the State', in *Church Congress Report* (1905) p. 190. Infra., p. 140.
24. *The Church and the Nation*, p. 72.
25. *Churches*, p. 45.
26. *Authority*, pp. 27 and 122.
27. *Holmes-Laski Letters*, p. 622.
28. 'The Pluralistic State', *28 The Philosophical Review* (1919) p. 566. Infra., p. 148.
29. H. A. Deane, *The Political Ideas of Harold J. Laski*, p. 19.
30. *Problem*, p. 23.
31. Op. cit., p. 84.
32. *Chaos*, p. 55.
33. In *Self Government* and in *Labour* Cole wrote of the state as nothing more that an association of consumers; in *Social Theory* he regarded this as *one* of the features of the state, while later in the same year he claimed in *Guild Socialism Restated* (sic) to have 'destroyed the idea that the State represents the consumer' (p. 120).
34. 'Conflicting Social Obligations', *15 Proceedings of the Aristotelian Society* (1914-15) p. 158.
35. *Principles of Social Reconstruction*, p. 58.
36. Ibid., p. 72.
37. *Democracy and Direct Action*, p. 6.
38. 'The Discredited State', in *The Political Quarterly*, Feb 1915, p. 101. But in a note to the article Barker added that the war was showing how loyalty to the state was still a powerful force.
39. *The Philosophical Foundations of English Socialism*, p. 86.
40. *Introduction to Contemporary Politics*, p. 69.
41. *Churches*, p. 92.
42. *The New State*, pp. 291 and 312.
43. 'Community is a Process' in *28 Philosophical Review*, p. 580.
44. *The New State*, p. 312.
45. Op cit., p. 86.
46. David Nicholls, 'Politics and Religion in Haiti', *3 Canadian Journal of Political Science*, Sep 1970.

6 AUTHORITY IN THE CHURCH

1. Clark Kerr, *Industrial Relations and the Liberal Pluralist*, p. 14.

2. *Law, Society and Industrial Justice*, p. 38; cf. also Grant McConnell in J. R. Pennock and J. W. Chapman (eds.), *Voluntary Associations*, p. 153.
3. Selznick, op. cit., p. 40.
4. *Du pape*, pp. 15-16.
5. *Fellowship*, p. 201; cf. also *Antichrist*, p. 263.
6. *Hopes*, p. 71, and *Churches*, p. 136.
7. *Churches*, pp. 151 and 237; also Figgis in G. K. A. Bell (ed.), *The Meaning of the Creed*, p. 193.
8. *The Church and the Future*, p. 120n; also Figgis, *The Gospel and Human Needs*, p. 137.
9. *Fellowship*, p. 188.
10. *Hopes*, p. 74.
11. *Fellowship*, p. 189. 'Each nation, partriarchate, diocese, parish, finally the individual Christian, all bear their part.' Ibid., pp. 202-3.
12. *Hopes*, p. 120.
13. Figgis in A. J. Mason *et al.*, *Our Place in Christendom*, p. 119.
14. The conciliar movement, 'stands for an incoate federalism and the rights of national groups, as against a centralising bureaucracy'. Ibid., p. 94.
15. F. Dvornik, *National Churches and the Church Universal*, p. 6.
16. Figgis was preparing a MS on Bossuet before he died in 1919. See also *Our Place in Christendom*, p. 122, and 'Some Recent Bossuet Literature', *18 Journal of Theological Studies* (1916-17) pp. 313f.
17. *Our Place in Christendom*, pp. 122f.
18. *Hopes* p. 80; cf; also *The Gospel and Human Needs* p. 137.
19. *Hopes*, pp. 59 and 63f.
20. *Our Place in Christendom*, p. 91.
21. Ibid., p. 140.
22. Newman, *A Letter Addressed to his Grace the Duke of Norfolk*, p. 66.
23. *Fellowship*, p. 55; cf. also P. T. Forsyth, *The Principle of Authority*, p. 400.
24. *Churches*, p. 154.
25. Sidgwick *The Ethics of Conformity and Subscription*, and 'The Ethics of Religious Conformity' and 'Clerical Veracity' in *Practical Ethics*.
26. L. Creighton, *Life and Letters of Mandell Creighton*, ii 347; Charles Gore, *The Basis of Anglican Fellowship*, p. 26; J. F. Bethune-Baker, *The Miracle of Christianity*; H. Rashdall, 'Professor Sidgwick on the Ethics of Religious Conformity: a Reply' in *7 The International Journal of Ethics* (1897) 137f; H. M. Gwatkin, *The Bishop of Oxford's Open Letter*; W. Sanday, *Bishop Gore's Challenge to Criticism*.
27. *The Church and the Future*, pp. 142-3.
28. See Acton, *The History of Freedom*, pp. xviif.
29. Op. cit., p. 145.
30. Figgis in Bell (ed.), *The Meaning of the Creed* p. 205.
31. *Fellowship*, p. 270.
32. *Hopes*, p. 120; *Fellowship*, pp. 168 and 155.
33. *Hopes*, p. 32.
34. *The Social Teaching of the Christian Churches*, i 329f. and ii 461f.

35. D. Warwick, 'The Centralisation of Ecclesiastical Authority: an Organisational Perspective', *Concilium*, Jan 1974, p. 109.
36. Ibid., p. 110.
37. Cf. K. Rahner, *Bishops: their Status and Function*, pp. 63f.
38. 'Pluralism in Theology and the Unity of the Church's Profession of Faith', *Concilium*, June 1969, p. 49.
39. Ibid., p. 50. Perhaps the period of the modernist movement at the beginning of the present century would be an exception to this.
40. Ibid., p. 56.
41. Ibid., p. 55.
42. 'Theology and Unity' 77 *Theology* (1974) pp. 4f. This 'inductive' approach to theology is clearly present in Schleiermacher and his followers, in George Tyrrell and many of his modernist contemporaries. Cf. also M. Wiles, *The Remaking of Christian Doctrine*.
43. Op. cit., p. 57. Whether this is wholly consistent with what Rahner says elsewhere about authority and the development of dogma is a complicated question. See Rahner *Theological Investigations*, i 39f and iv 3f. Cf. David Nicholls, 'Developing Doctrines and Changing Beliefs' *19 Scottish Journal of Theology* (1966) pp. 280f. and 'Authority and the Development of Doctrine' 63 *Theology* (1960) pp. 136f.
44. 'Pluralism in Theology . . .', p. 53. Cf. W. M. Thompson 'Rahner's Theology of Pluralism', *The Ecumenist*, Jan-Feb 1973, p. 20.
45. 'The Spirit of Private Government' 52 *American Political Science Review* (1958) p. 754.

7 SOME INSTITUTIONAL CONSEQUENCES OF PLURALISM

1. *Divine Right*, p. 199.
2. *Problem*, p. 108.
3. Ibid., p. 69n.
4. *Churches*, p. 114.
5. Ibid., p. 112.
6. *Fellowship*, pp. 100f. For recent discussions of secularisation and religious pluralism see P. Berger and T. Luckmann, 'Secularisation and Pluralism' in *2 International Yearbook for the Sociology of Religion* (1966) 74; also the first volume of ibid. (1965) on the theme 'Religious Pluralism and Social Structure'; L. Shiner, 'The Meaning of Secularisation', ibid., 3 (1967) 52f; S. S. Acquaviva, *L'eclissi del sacro nella civiltà industriale;* H. Cox, *The Secular City;* J. B. Metz, *Zur Theologie der Welt*, etc.
7. Introduction to D. Nicholls (ed.), *Church and State in Britain since 1820*, pp. 13f. And supra., pp. 13f.
8. *The Will to Freedom*, p. 301.
9. *The Gospel and Human Needs*, p. 11.
10. *Fellowship*, p. 146.
11. *The Church and the Nation*, p. 277.
12. *The Cambridge Review*, 3 Feb 1915 179. G. Le Bras has argued that religious belief and practice, which has become less extensive in present-day France than in earlier days, has become more intensive and informed. 'Déchristianisation: mot fallacieux', *10 Social Compass* (1963) pp. 445f.

13. B. Mitchell, *Law, Morality and Religion in a Secular Society*, pp. 1 and 136.
14. P. Devlin, *The Enforcement of Morals*, and H. L. A. Hart, *Law, Liberty and Morality*.
15. Op. cit., p. 136.
16. H. M. Relton, *Church and State*, p. 18.
17. G. L. Prestige, *The Life of Charles Gore*, p. 352.
18. Church Information Office, *Church and State*, paras. 117f.
19. Cf. S. T. Glass, *The Responsible Society*.
20. Cf. particularly K. Coates and T. Topham, *Workers' Control.*
21. J. E. F. Mann *et al.*, *The Real Democracy;* also H. Belloc and C. Chesterton, *The Party System;* H. Belloc, *The Servile State;* P. Derrick, *Lost Property*.
22. 'Notes and Comments', in *29 The Political Quarterly* (1958) p. 4.

8 CONCLUSION

1. *A Pluralistic Universe*, p. 79.
2. Ibid., p. 321.
3. J. W. Scott, *Syndicalism and Philosophical Realism*, p. 161.
4. *Quality of Life in the Americas*, p. 27. I have discussed American pluralist theories in a little more detail in *Three Varieties of Pluralism*.
5. Op. cit., p. 231.
6. Ibid., pp. 225 and 227.
7. Ibid., p. 155n.
8. Eisenhower, however, saw this military-industrial complex as a challenge to the authority of the government, while Mills saw the government as a part of the power elite.
9. *The Decline of American Pluralism*, p. 2; cf. also W. E. Connolly (ed.), *The Bias of Pluralism*.
10. *The Poverty of Liberalism*, p. 159.
11. D. Baskin, 'American Pluralism' in *32 Journal of Politics* (1970) p. 85.
12. Ibid.
13. R. P. Wolff, op. cit., p. 151.
14. J. S. Furnivall, *Colonial Policy and Practice*, pp. 297f; and 'Some Problems of Tropical Economy', in R. Hinden (ed.) *Fabian Colonial Essays*, pp. 167f. I have considered the idea of social and cultural pluralism in greater detail in *Three Varieties of Pluralism*.
15. Cf. V. Rubin (ed.), *Social and Cultural Pluralism in the Caribbean*, and L. Kuper and M. G. Smith (eds.), *Pluralism in Africa.* There is a useful bibliography in the last-mentioned book on pp. 491f.
16. *Class and Class Conflict in Industrial Society*, p. 316.
17. R. Bendix in his English translation of G. Simmel, *The Web of Group Affiliations*.
18. T. M. Knox and Z. A. Pelczynski (eds.), *Hegel's Political Writings*, p. 155.
19. Cf. David Nicholls, 'East Indians and Black Power in Trinidad' *12 Race* (1971) pp. 443f.
20. Cambridge University Library, Add. MSS 5011:235.

Legal Cases Cited

A. G. *v* Great Northern Railway Co., 1 Drewry and Smales Rep. 154.
Barwick *v* English Joint Stock Bank, L. R. 2 Exch. 259.
Cornford *v* Carlton Bank, [1899] 1 Q.B. 392.
D.P.P. *v* Kent and Sussex Contractors Ltd, [1944] K.B. 146.
Edwards *v* Midland Railway Co., [1881] 50 L.J. Q.B. 281.
General Assembly of the Free Church of Scotland *v* Overtoun (Lord),
    [1904] A.C. 515.
Henderson *v* Midland Railway Co., [1871] 24 L.T.N.S. 881.
Kedroff *v* St Nicholas Cathedral, 344 U.S. Sup. Ct. 1952 94.
Kent *v* Courage & Co. Ltd, [1890] 55 J.P. 264.
Osborne *v* Amalgamated Society of Railway Servants, [1910] A.C. 87.
R. *v* Cory Bros. & Co. Ltd, [1927] 1 K.B. 810.
R. *v* I.C.R. Haulage Ltd, [1944] K.B. 551.
Salomon *v* Salomon & Co., [1897] A.C. 22.
Stevens *v* Midland Counties Railway Co., 10 Exch. 352.
Sutton's Hospital Case, [1613] 10 Co. Rep.
Taff Vale Railway Co. *v* Amalgamated Society of Railway Servants,
    [1901] A.C. 426.

Appendix A
The Church and the Secular Theory of the State[1]

J. N. FIGGIS

There are two great tasks before the Church. Both are predominantly intellectual. Yet without them practical work must first become hollow and then disappear. Of these tasks the former has been treated — apologetics proper. We need to convince the individual that the Christian faith is not an excusable survival among the vulgar, not an emotional eccentricity of the cultivated, but is at once the condition and the consequence of personal and intellectual development, where it is complete. Education in its full sense, the making of a man, does not tolerate the faith of the Cross; it postulates it. The culture of the whole being is a 'schoolmaster to bring men to Christ'. To show this is our first and greatest task. It is the supreme achievement of Mandell Creighton, that he witnessed to the truth by what he was.

It is, however, with the second and the smaller of these tasks that this paper deals — the semi-political one of investigating the place of the self-conscious Church in the modern State. We have to show that the Church may claim a due independence, because it is a life not a contrivance; an organism not an organisation. Its claim to recognition is disinterested and serves the whole community — Christian and non-Christian. In a word, when the Church asks the State to acknowledge that it has real powers for developing itself, it is asking not for a privilege to be conceded, but for the facts to be realized. The Church is to fight not for its own hand, but for what is *true* about human life in society.

What is the enemy which we have to face?

'There are no rights but the rights of the State, there can be no authority but the authority of the republic.' These

are the words of M. Combes anent the dissolution of the
Concordat in France. In a couple of phrases they concentrate
the notions of our adversaries. That there may be a juristic
sense in which these words are true, I do not deny. Nothing is
gained by ignoring facts. Legally, the State could establish
Mohammedanism to-morrow — or rather in the next session
of Parliament. But if we regard as a practical maxim a
description of facts or an ideal for the future, the statement
of M. Combes has no other merit but that of being indis-
putably false. Firstly, we may say that in England nobody
now — unless a few absolute Socialists — believes it to be
practically true of individuals. There are certain rights such as
those for discussion, contract, and fair trial which have become *real* for all. Legally, indeed, they can be treated as the
grant of the State. Actually, they are the result of age-long
struggles and the expression of the English character. What
we have now to secure is the liberty and power of self-
development of *Societies* other than the State. It is in regard
to such societies — to the Church, in fact — that for the next
two generations or more the issue is going to be joined. The
battle will be inevitable and terrific between those who
believe and those who do not believe, that 'there are no rights
but the rights of the State, there can be no authority but the
authority of the republic'.

Let us try and see a little more clearly what it means.
In his campaign against the religious orders, M. Combes
declared that to take vows of obedience was to encroach
upon the civil power, and to surrender what no one has a
right to surrender. This dots the 'i's' a little. Take it in
conjunction with the proposal — of another anti-clerical — to
prohibit to religious uses those cathedrals which are the glory
of France, and the symbol of the illustrious lineage of its
people; and we shall see what the maxim expanded in practice may come to mean. They want, as they said, to create a
unité morale through the State, the atmosphere of all education, the main source of the idea of duty. You can read
more in the volume *Une Campagne Laique* of M. Combes. Dr
Clifford's Letters are also illuminating. I mention these because issues are clear in France, without desiring to prejudge
the question whether this attack be not the just nemesis of

ultramontanism. The point is not what the French Church may or may not deserve; but that M. Combes stands for a certain notion of human society, and that notion is *false*. Here things are more confused, and Englishmen always more really tolerant even when they delude themselves into the belief that they are bigots. Yet the same idea is dominant in this country to-day, and it has to be met. And the only way possible to conquer a false idea is to put the true one into people's minds. 'Ideas rule the world, in the long run.'

What is the real objection to undenominationalism? It is not un-Christian. There is no theoretic reason why an undenominational system should not teach that love to Jesus of which all dogma is the inadequate intellectual expression and every Christian institution the imperfect realization. It might, indeed, be merely a matter of expediency whether or not an undenominational solution of the education problem be not possible. But undenominationalism (and secularism too) as a universal principle means more than this. It means the denial of religion except as an individual luxury or a State-boon. The religious society is to be nothing — except to the fortunate classes — any more than the family is to pauper children in a workhouse. That the Church should be the home of the soul from its baptism is denied. The only home is the State. The State is to consider individuals only — and in no way to recognise churches for the educational period of the great majority of its citizens. To assert against this doctrine the rights of the parent, i.e., of the family as the unit instead of the individual, may be expedient, but it is not enough. What we must assert, are bound to assert, cannot help asserting if we have thought out our principles is this. The Church *has* real rights and true authority over all its members the moment they become such. The parent must bring the child, it is true. But the moment anyone has joined a church (or a club for that matter), he is not only John Smith, but an integral part of a society with a life of its own. We are fighting no selfish battle, advocating no private cause. It is public freedom that we want. We say that the world is *not*, as a fact, composed of a few vast unities known as States, set over against crowds of isolated individuals; but is a society of societies, each and all with rights, liberty and life of their own.

We do not need to deny the due rights of the civil power, as the guardian of property and interpreter of contract. We shall do no good by claiming for the Church powers which it is either inexpedient or unfair for it to exercise. We need enquiry. We must know the limits as well as the province of the Church within the modern State. I merely suggest the problem. What does the self-conscious life of the religious society mean in relation to affairs to-day? What is its essence? Only as knowing this shall we know what we must claim and where we are bound to stop. It is a new problem. In the mediaeval world, and for a long while after the Reformation, Church and State appeared as merely different departments of the same institution. Of course they quarrelled, as Government departments do. Even soldiers and civilians have been known to quarrel in the year of grace 1905. Now, however, this has ceased even in appearance. What we have to secure is our corporate existence, our real life functioning inside a State, itself made up of complex elements and tolerating all religions. The tolerant State is the true State. The uniform State of the past was founded on a lie. Religious persecution is fundamentally un-Christian. We are suffering for the sins of our fathers. But the State has yet to learn that she must tolerate not merely individual liberty but the religious society, must know that its life is real and must develop, and cannot (not *must* not) be stopped. This is our task; it is hard, but it is high. We have to do with the real facts of human society, not with prescriptive claims or traditional rights. We have the future with us, not merely the past.

Establishment cannot save us. Only this year our most eminent philosophic jurist expressed something like horror that in such a matter as divorce the clergy of the State Church should be permitted to have a different view of morals from that of the State.[2]

Disestablishment will not deliver us. France shows that. Only the truth can make us free.

The question, be it observed, is not the theological one, 'What is the Divine authority or nature of the Church?' but the political, 'What rights has the religious society which the State is bound to acknowledge on pain of being false to itself?'

Scotland has given us an example. In the case of the United Free Church, the most august Court of Judicature in the world found itself unable to allow that a religious community had any real life of its own, in fact was more than a company formed upon certain articles under the aegis of the State. No reasoning of Mr Haldane could convince those luminaries that the Church, so far as the law was concerned, could be anything more than a body of trustees. The idea of inherent corporate life they rejected. Such was the law; not so the facts. Even through a moribund and paralytic Parliament was driven a statute of far-reaching import to prevent *summum jus* being *summa injuria.* The fact is, that to deny to smaller societies a real life and meaning, a personality, in fact, is not anti-clerical, or illiberal, or unwise, or oppressive — it is *untrue.* And 'all the king's horses and all the king's men' cannot make that true which is untrue. The House of Lords cannot do it. Even the Roman Empire, with the mediaeval Papacy thrown in, the *fons et origo mali* cannot do it; because it is impossible. And we shall win.

But we shall not win yet. It may be a thousand years before we do or only a generation. It does not matter. We shall not win without a struggle — a struggle in which hard thought and patience must be ours; and that charity that comes of being sure. We need a clear intellectual knowledge of principles, and the will to fight for essentials — but for nothing else. This work — that of securing the liberty and real life of societies within the huge and complex modern State — will not be done by irresponsible chatter or by mere sentimentalism, in all ages the danger of religion. It will not be done by treating the Church of England as a *pis aller*, just good enough not to desert — so long as you can disobey the bishop. It cannot be done by individualist caprice masquerading as Catholic custom. Least of all will it be done by uncritical appeals to the *Corpus Juris Canonici*, a code relative to the conditions of mediaeval Europe, saturated with Papalism, and its earlier portions steeped in forgery.

Done, however, the work must and shall be, if the Church is not to vanish into a royal benevolent fund or dissolve into an academic debating society. We must have no want of charity or calumnies against Dissent, even though it should appear bigoted or refuse to understand us; if we do not know better, why are we Churchmen? We must not mistake rapid for wise action, or violent language for firmness. Ours must be perfect tolerance, but also entire conviction; unwearied thought and courage immovable; above all, the faith — the real faith that is strong and 'endures as seeing Him Who is invisible'. And then we are bound to win — we cannot help it — for it is we and not our adversaries, who are for truth and freedom in human society.

Notes

1. From *Church Congress Report* (1905) pp. 189f.
2. See A. V. Dicey, *Law and Public Opinion in England*.

Appendix B
The Pluralistic State[1]

H. J. LASKI

Every student of politics must begin his researches with humble obeisance to the work of Aristotle; and therein, I take it, he makes confession of the inspiration and assistance he has had from the effort of philosophers. Indeed, if one took only the last century of intellectual history, names like Hegel, Green, and Bosanquet must induce in him a certain sense of humility. For the direction of his analysis has been given its perspective by their thought. The end his effort must achieve has been by no other thinkers so clearly or so wisely defined.

Yet the philosophic interpretation of politics has suffered from one serious weakness. It is rather with *staatslehre* than with *politik* that it has concerned itself. Ideals and forms have provided the main substance of its debates. So that even if, as with Hegel and Green, it has had the battles of the market-place most clearly in mind, it has somehow, at least ultimately, withdrawn itself from the arena of hard facts to those remoter heights where what a good Platonist has called[2] the 'pure instance' of the state may be dissected. Nor has it seen political philosophy sufficiently outside the area of its own problems. Aristotle apart, its weakness has lain exactly in those minutiae of psychology which, collectively, are all-important to the student of administration. Philosophy seems, in politics at least, to take too little thought for the categories of space and time.

The legal attitude has been impaired by a somewhat similar limitation. The lawyer, perhaps of necessity, has concerned himself not with right but with rights, and his consequent preoccupation with the problem of origins, the place of ultimate reference, has made him, at least to the interested outsider, unduly eager to confound the legally ancient with the politically justifiable. One might even make out a case for the assertion that the lawyer is the head and centre of our modern trouble; for the monistic theory of the state goes back, in its scientific statement, to Jean Bodin. The latter became the spiritual parent of Hobbes, and thence, through Bentham, the ancestor of Austin. On Austin I will make no comment here; though a reference to an ingenious equation of Maitland's may perhaps be pardoned.[3]

It is with the lawyers that the problem of the modern state originates as an actual theory; for the lawyer's formulae have been rather amplified than denied by the philosophers. Upon the historic events which surround their effort I would say one word, since it is germane to the argument I have presently to make. We must ceaselessly remember that the monistic theory of the state was born in an age of crisis and that each period of its revivification has synchronised with some momentous event which has signalised a change in the distribution of political power. Bodin, as is well known, was of that party which, in an age of religious warfare, asserted, lest it perish in an alien battle, the supremacy of the state.[4] Hobbes sought the means of order in a period when King and Parliament battled for the balance of power. Bentham published his *Fragment* on the eve of the Declaration of Independence; and Adam Smith, in the same year, was outlining the programme of another and profounder revolution. Hegel's philosophy was the outcome of a vision of German multiplicity destroyed by the unity of France. Austin's book was conceived when the middle classes of France and England had, in their various ways, achieved the conquest of a state hitherto but partly open to their ambition.

It seems of peculiar significance that each assertion of the monistic theory should have this background. I cannot stay here to disentangle the motives through which men so different in character should have embraced a theory as similar in substance. The result, with all of them, is to assert the supremacy of the state over all other institutions. Its primary organs have the first claim upon the allegiance of men; and Hobbes's insistence[5] that corporations other than the state are but the manifestations of disease is perhaps the best example of its ruthless logic. Hobbes and Hegel apart, the men I have noted were lawyers; and they were seeking a means whereby the source of power may have some adequate justification. Bentham, of course, at no point beatified the state; though zeal for it is not wanting in the earlier thinkers or in Hegel. What, I would urge, the lawyers did was to provide a foundation for the moral superstructure of the philosophers. It was by the latter that the monistic state was elevated from the plane of logic to the plane of ethics. Its rights then became matter of right. Its sovereignty became spiritualised into moral preëminence.

The transition is simple enough. The state is today the one compulsory form of association;[6] and for more than two thousand years we have been taught that its purpose is the perfect life. It thus seems to acquire a flavor of generality which is absent from all other institutions. It becomes instinct with an universal interest to which, as it appears, no other association may without inaccuracy lay claim. Its sovereignty thus seems to represent the protection of the universal aspect of men — what Rousseau called the common good — against the intrusion of more private aspects at the hands of which it might otherwise suffer humiliation. The state is an absorptive animal; and there are few more amazing tracts of history than that which records its triumphs over the challenge of competing groups. There seems, at least today, no certain method of escape from its demands. Its conscience is supreme over any private conception of good the individual may hold. It sets the terms upon which the lives of trade-unions may be lived. It dictates their doctrine to churches; and, in England at least, it was a state tribunal which, as Lord Westbury said, dismissed hell with costs.[7] The area of its enterprise has consistently grown until today there is no field of human activity over which, in some degree, its pervading influence may not be detected.

But it is at this point pertinent to inquire what exact meaning is to be attached to an institution so vital as this. With one definition only I shall trouble you. 'A state,' writes Mr Zimmern,[8] 'can be defined, in legal language, as a territory over which there is a government claiming unlimited authority.' The definition, indeed, is not quite correct; for no government in the United States could claim, though it might usurp, unlimited power. But it is a foible of the lawyers to insist upon the absence of legal limit to the authority of the state; and it is, I think, ultimately clear that the monistic theory is bound up with some such assumption. But it is exactly here that our main difficulty begins to emerge. The state, as Mr Zimmern here points out, must act through organs; and, in the analysis of its significance, it is upon government that we must concentrate our main attention.[9]

Legally, no one can deny that there exists in every state some organ whose authority is unlimited. But that legality is no more than a fiction of logic. No man has stated more clearly than Professor Dicey[10] the sovereign character of the King in Parliament; no man has been also so quick to point out the practical limits to this supremacy. And if logic is thus out of accord with the facts of life the obvious question to be asked is why unlimited authority may be claimed. The answer, I take it, is reducible to the belief that government expresses the largest aspect of man and is thus entitled to institutional expression of the area covered by its interests. A history, of course, lies back of that attitude, the main part of which would be concerned with the early struggle of the modern state to be born. Nor do I think the logical character of the doctrine has all the sanction claimed for it. It is only with the decline of theories of natural law that Parliament becomes the complete master of its destinies. And the internal limits which the jurist is driven to admit prove, on examination, to be the main problem for consideration.

There are many different angles from which this claim to unlimited authority may be proved inadequate. That government is the most important of institutions few, except theocrats, could be found to deny; but that its importance warrants the monistic assumption herein implied raises far wider questions. The test, I would urge, is not an *a priori* statement of claim. Nothing has led us farther on the wrong path than the simple teleological terms in which Aristotle stated his conclusions. For when we say that political institutions aim at the good life, we need to know not only the meaning of good, but also those who are to achieve it, and the methods by which it is to be attained. What, in fact, we have to do is to study the way in which this monistic theory has worked; for our judgment upon it must depend upon its consequences to the mass of men and women. I would not trouble you unduly with history. But it is worth while to bear in mind that this worship of state-unity is almost entirely the offspring of the Reformation and therein, most largely, an adaptation of the practice of the medieval church. The fear of variety was not, in its early days, an altogether unnatural thing. Challenged from within and from without, uniformity seemed the key to self-preservation.[11] But when the internal history of the state is examined, its supposed unity of purpose and of effort sinks, with acquaintance, into nothingness. What in fact confronts us is a complex of interests; and between not few of them ultimate reconciliation is impossible. We cannot, for example, harmonise the modern secular state with a Roman Church based upon the principles of the Encyclical of 1864; nor can we find the basis of enduring collaboration between trade-unions aiming at the control of industry through the destruction of capitalistic organisation and the upholders of capitalism. Historically, we always find that any system of government is dominated by those who at the time wield economic power; and what they mean by 'good' is, for the most part, the preservation of their own interests. Perhaps I put it too crudely; refined analysis would, maybe, suggest that they are limited by the circle of the ideas to which their interests would at the first instance give rise. The history of England in the period of the Industrial Revolution is perhaps the most striking example of this truth. To suggest, for instance, that the government of the younger Pitt was, in its agricultural policy, actuated by some conception of public welfare which was equal as between squire and laborer, is, in the light of the evidence so superbly discussed by Mr and Mrs Hammond, utterly impossible.[12] There is nowhere and at no time assurance of that consistent generality of motive in the practice of government which theory would suppose it to possess.

We cannot, that is to say, at any point, take for granted the motives of governmental policy, with the natural implication that we must erect safeguards against their abuse. These, I venture to think, the monistic theory of the state at no point, in actual practice, supplies. For its insistence on unlimited authority in the governmental organ makes over to it the immense power that comes from the possession of legality. What, in the stress of conflict, this comes to mean is the attribution of inherent rightness to acts of government. These are somehow taken, and that with but feeble regard to their actual substance, to be acts of the community. Something that, for want of a better term, we call the communal conscience, is supposed to want certain things. We rarely inquire either how it comes to want them or to need them. We simply know that the government enforces the demand so made and that the individual or group is expected to give way before them. Yet it may well happen, as we have sufficiently seen in our experience, that the individual or the group may be right. And it is difficult to see how a policy which thus penalises all dissent, at least in active form, from government, can claim affinity with freedom. For freedom, as Mr Graham Wallas has finely said,[13] implies the chance of continuous initiative. But the ultimate implication of the monistic state in a society so complex as our own is the transference of that freedom from ordinary men to their rulers.

I cannot here dwell upon the more technical results of this doctrine, more particularly on the absence of liability for the faults of government that it has involved.[14] But it is in some such background as this that the pluralistic theory of the state takes its origin. It agrees with Mr. Zimmern that a state is a territorial society divided into government and subjects, but it differs, as you will observe, from his definition in that it makes no assumptions as to the authority a government should possess. And the reason for this fact is simply that it is consistently experimentalist in temper. It realized that the state has a history and it is unwilling to assume that we have today given to it any permanence of form. There is an admirable remark of Tocqueville's on this point which we too little bear in mind.[15] And if it be deemed necessary to dignify this outlook by antiquity we can, I think, produce great names as its sponsors. At least it could be shown that the germs of our protest are in men like Nicholas of Cusa, like Althusius, Locke, and Royer-Collard.

It thus seems that we have a twofold problem. The monistic state is an hierarchical structure in which power is, for

ultimate purposes, collected at a single centre. The advocates
of pluralism are convinced that this is both administratively
incomplete and ethically inadequate. You will observe that I
have made no reference here to the lawyer's problem. Nor do
I deem it necessary; for when we are dealing, as the lawyer
deals, with sources of ultimate reference, the questions are no
more difficult, perhaps I should also add, no easier, than
those arising under the conflict of jurisdictions in a federal
state.

It is with other questions that we are concerned. Let us
note, in the first place, the tendency in the modern state for
men to become the mere subjects of administration. It is
perhaps as yet too early to insist, reversing a famous generali-
sation of Sir Henry Maine, that the movement of our society
is from contract to status; but there is at least one sense in
which that remark is significant. Amid much vague enthu-
siasm for the thing itself, every observer must note a decline
in freedom. What we most greatly need is to beware lest we
lose that sense of spontaneity which enabled Aristotle to
define citizenship as the capacity to rule not less than to be
ruled in turn.[16] We believe that this can best be achieved in a
state of which the structure is not hierarchical but coordinate, in which, that is to say, sovereignty is partitioned upon
some basis of function. For the division of power makes men
more apt to responsibility than its accumulation. A man, or
even a legislature that is overburdened with a multiplicity of
business, will not merely neglect that which he ought to do;
he will, in actual experience, surrender his powers into the
hands of forceful interests which know the way to compel his
attention. He will treat the unseen as non-existent and the
inarticulate as contented. The result may, indeed, be revolution; but experience suggests that it is more likely to be the
parent of a despotism.

Nor is this all. Such a system must needs result in a futile
attempt to apply equal and uniform methods to varied and
unequal things. Every administrator has told us of the effort
to arrive at an intellectual routine; and where the problems of
government are as manifold as at present that leads to an
assumption of similarity which is rarely borne out by the
facts. The person who wishes to govern America must know

that he cannot assume identity of conditions in North and South, East and West. He must, that is to say, assume that his first duty is not to assert a greatest common measure of equality but to prove it. That will, I suggest, lead most critical observers to perceive that the unit with which we are trying to deal is too large for effective administration. The curiosities, say of the experiment in North Dakota, are largely due to this attempt on the part of predominating interests to neglect vital differences of outlook. Such differences, moreover, require a sovereignty of their own to express the needs they imply. Nor must we neglect the important fact that in an area like the United States the individual will too often get lost in its very vastness. He gets a sense of impotence as a political factor of which the result is a failure properly to estimate the worth of citizenship. I cannot stay to analyse the result of that mistaken estimate. I can only say here that I am convinced that it is the nurse of social corruption.

Administratively, therefore, we need decentralisation; or, if you like, we need to revivify the conception of federalism which is the great contribution of America to political science. But we must not think of federalism today merely in the old spatial terms. It applies not less to functions than to territories. It applies not less to the government of the cotton industry, or of the civil service, than it does to the government of Kansas and Rhode Island. Indeed, the greatest lesson the student of government has to learn is the need for him to understand the significance for politics of industrial structure and, above all, the structure of the trade-union movement.[17] The main factor in political organization that we have to recover is the factor of consent, and here trade-union federalism has much to teach us. It has found, whether the unit be a territorial one like the average local, or an industrial like that envisaged by the shop-steward movement in England, units sufficiently small to make the individual feel significant in them. What, moreover, this development of industrial organization has done is to separate the processes of production and consumption in such fashion as to destroy, for practical purposes, the unique sovereignty of a territorial parliament. It is a nice question for the upholders of the

monistic theory to debate as to where the effective sovereignty of America lay in the controversy over the Adamson
law; or to consider what is meant by the vision of that
consultative industrial body which recent English experience
seems likely, in the not distant future, to bring into being.[18]

The facts, I suggest, are driving us towards an effort at the
partition of power. The evidence for that conclusion you can
find on all sides. The civil services of England and France are
pressing for such a reorganization.[19] It is towards such a
conclusion that what we call too vaguely the labor movement
has directed its main energies.[20] We are in the midst of a new
movement for the conquest of self-government. It finds its
main impulse in the attempt to disperse the sovereign power
because it is realised that where administrative organization is
made responsive to the actual associations of men, there is a
greater chance not merely of efficiency but of freedom also.
That is why, in France, there has been for some time a
vigorous renewal of that earlier effort of the sixties in which
the great Odillon-Barrot did his noblest work;[21] and it does
not seem unlikely that some reconstruction of the ancient
provinces will at last compensate for the dangerous absorp-
tiveness of Paris. The British House of Commons has debated
federalism as the remedy for its manifold ills;[22] and the
unused potentialities of German decentralisation may lead to
the results so long expected now that the deadening pressure
of Prussian domination has been withdrawn. We are learning,
as John Stuart Mill pointed out in an admirable passage,[23]
that 'all the facilities which a government enjoys of access to
information, all the means which it possesses of remunera-
ting, and therefore of commanding, the best available talent
in the market, are not an equivalent for the one great dis-
advantage of an inferior interest in the result'. For we now
know that the consequent of that inferior interest is the
consistent degradation of freedom.[24]

I have spoken of the desire for genuine responsibility and
the direction in which it may be found for administrative
purposes. To this aspect the ethical side of political pluralism
stands in the closest relation. Fundamentally, it is a denial
that a law can be explained merely as a command of the
sovereign for the simple reason that it denies, ultimately, the

sovereignty of anything save right conduct. The philosophers since, particularly, the time of T. H. Green, have told us insistently that the state is based upon will; though they have too little examined the problem of what will is most likely to receive obedience. With history behind us, we are compelled to conclude that no such will can by definition be a good will; and the individual must therefore, whether by himself or in concert with others, pass judgment upon its validity by examining its substance. That, it is clear enough, makes an end of the sovereignty of the state in its classical conception. It puts the state's acts — practically, as I have pointed out, the acts of its primary organ, government — on a moral parity with the acts of any other association. It gives to the judgments of the state exactly the power they inherently possess by virtue of their moral content, and no other. If the English state should wish, as in 1776, to refuse colonial freedom; if Prussia should choose to embark upon a Kulturkampf; if any state, to take the decisive instance, should choose to embark upon war; in each case there is no *a priori* rightness about its policy. You and I are part of the leverage by which that policy is ultimately enacted. It therefore becomes a moral duty on our part to examine the foundations of state-action. The last sin in politics is unthinking acquiescence in important decisions.

I have elsewhere dealt with the criticism that this view results in anarchy.[25] What it is more profitable here to examine is its results in our scheme of political organization. It is, in the first place, clear that there are no demands upon our allegiance except the demands of what we deem right conduct. Clearly, in such an aspect, we need the means of ensuring that we shall know right when we see it. Here, I would urge, the problem of rights becomes significant. For the duties of citizenship cannot be fulfilled, save under certain conditions; and it is necessary to ensure the attainment of those conditions against the encroachments of authority. I cannot here attempt any sort of detail; but it is obvious enough that freedom of speech,[26] a living wage, an adequate education, a proper amount of leisure, the power to combine for social effort, are all of them integral to citizenship. They are natural rights in the sense that without them the purpose of the state cannot be fulfilled. They are natural also in the sense that they do not depend upon the state for their validity. They are inherent in the eminent worth of human personality. Where they are denied, the state clearly destroys whatever claims it has upon the loyalty of men.

Rights such as these are necessary to freedom because without them man is lost in a world almost beyond the reach of his understanding. We have put them outside the power of the state to traverse; and this again must mean a limit upon its sovereignty. If you ask what guarantee exists against their destruction in a state where power is distributed, the answer, I think, is that only in such a state have the masses of men the opportunity to understand what is meant by their denial. It is surely, for example, significant that the movement for the revival of what we broadly term natural law should derive its main strength from organized trade-unionism. It is hardly less important that among those who have perceived the real significant of the attitude of labor in the Taff Vale and Osborne cases should have been a high churchman most deeply concerned with the restoration of the church.[27] That is what coordinate organization will above all imply, and its main value is the fact that what, otherwise, must strike us most in the modern state is the inert receptiveness of the multitude. Every student of politics knows well enough what this means. Most would, on analysis, admit that its dissipation is mainly dependent upon an understanding of social mechanisms now largely hidden from the multitude. The only hopeful way of breaking down this inertia is by the multiplication of centres of authority. When a man is trained to service in a trade-union, he cannot avoid seeing how that activity is related to the world outside. When he gets on a school-committee, the general problems of education begin to unfold themselves before him. Paradoxically, indeed, we may say that a consistent decentralisation is the only effective cure for an undue localism. That is because institutions with genuine power become ethical ideas and thus organs of genuine citizenship. But if the Local Government Board, or the Prefect, sit outside, the result is a balked disposition of which the results are psychologically well known. A man may obtain some compensation for his practical exclusion from the inwardness of politics by devotion to golf. But I doubt whether the compensation is what is technically termed sublimation, and it almost always results in social loss.

Here, indeed, is where the main superiority of the pluralistic state is manifest. For the more profoundly we analyse the psychological characteristics of its opposite, the less adequate does it seem relative to the basic impulses of men. And this, after all, is the primary need to satisfy. It was easy enough for Aristotle to make a fundamental division between masters and men and adapt his technique to the demands of the former; but it was a state less ample than a moderate-sized city that he had in mind. It was simple for Hobbes to assume the inherent badness of men and the consequent need of making government strong, lest their evil nature bring it to ruin; yet even he must have seen, what our own generation has emphasized, that the strength of governments consists only in the ideas of which they dispose. It was even simple for Bentham to insist on the ruling motive of self-interest; but he wrote before it had become clear that altruism was an instinct implied in the existence of the herd. We know at least that the data are more complex. Our main business has become the adaptation of our institutions to a variety of impulses with the knowledge that we must at all costs prevent their inversion. In the absence of such transmutation what must mainly impress us is the wastage upon which our present system is builded. The executioner, as Maistre said, is the corner-stone of our society. But it is because we refuse to release the creative energies of men.

After all, our political systems must be judged not merely by the ends they serve, but also by the way in which they serve those ends. The modern state provides a path whereby a younger Pitt may control the destinies of a people; it even gives men of leisure a field of passionate interest to cultivate. But the humbler man is less fortunate in the avenues we afford; and if we have record of notable achievement after difficult struggle, we are too impressed by the achievement to take due note of the anguish upon which it is too often founded. This, it may be remarked, is the touchstone by which the major portion of our institutions will be tested in the future; and I do not think we can be unduly certain that they will stand the test. The modern state, at bottom, is too much an historic category not to change its nature with the advent of new needs.

Those new needs, it may be added, are upon us, and the future of our civilization most largely depends upon the temper in which we confront them. Those who take refuge in the irrefutable logic of the sovereign state may sometimes take thought that for many centuries of medieval history the very notion of sovereignty was unknown. I would not seek unduly to magnify those far-off times; but it is worth while to remember that no thoughts were dearer to the heart of medieval thinkers than ideals of right and justice. Shrunken and narrow, it may be, their fulfillment often was; but that was not because they did not know how to dream. Our finely articulated structure is being tested by men who do not know what labor and thought have gone into its building. It is a cruder test they will apply. Yet it is only by seeking to understand their desires that we shall be able worthily to meet it.

Notes

1. From 28 *Philosophical Review* (1919) 562ff.
2. Barker, *Political Thought in England from Herbert Spencer to Today*, pp. 68f.
3. Cf. *The Life of F. W. Maitland*, by H. A. L. Fisher, p. 117.
4. The background of his book has recently been exhaustively outlined by Roger Chauviré in his *Jean Bodin* (Paris, 1916), esp. pp. 312f.
5. *Leviathan*, chap. xliv.
6. I say today; for it is important to remember that, for the Western World, this was true of the Church until the Reformation.
7. A. W. Benn, *History of English Rationalism in the Nineteenth Century*, vol. ii, p. 133.
8. *Nationality and Government*, p. 56.
9. Cf. my *Authority in the Modern State*, pp. 26ff.
10. Cf. *The Law of the Constitution* (8th ed.), pp. 37ff.
11. Cf. Professor McIlwain's introduction to his edition of the *Political Works of James I*, and my comment thereon, *Pol. Sci. Quarterly*, vol. 34, p. 290.
12. See their brilliant volume, *The Village Laborer* (1911).
13. Cf. his article in the *New Statesman*, Sept. 25, 1915. I owe my

knowledge of this winning definition to Mr A. E. Zimmern's *Nationality and Government*, p. 57.

14. Cf. my paper on the Responsibility of the State in England, 32 *Harv. L. Rev.*, p. 447.
15. *Souvenirs*, p. 102.
16. *Politics*, bk. iii, c.1, 1275a.
17. A book that would do for the English-speaking world what M. Paul-Boncour did twenty years ago for France in his *Fédéralisme Économique* would be of great service.
18. See the *Report of the Provisional Joint Committee of the Industrial Conference*, London, 1919.
19. See my *Authority in the Modern State*, chap. v.
20. Cf. Cole, *Self-Government in Industry*, passim, esp. chap. iii.
21. Odillon-Barrot, *De la centralization.* [sic]
22. *Parliamentary Debates*, June 4th and 5th, 1919.
23. *Principles of Political Economy* (2nd ed.), vol. ii, p. 181.
24. On all this, cf. my *Problem of Administrative Areas* (Smith College Studies, vol. iv, no. 1).
25. *Authority in the Modern State*, pp. 93-4.
26. Cf. the brilliant article of my colleague, Professor Z. Chafee, Jr., in 32 *Harv. L. Rev.*, 932f.
27. J. Neville Figgis, *Churches in the Modern State*. The recent death of Dr Figgis is an irreparable blow to English scholarship.

Appendix C
Moral Personality and Legal Personality[1]

F. W. MAITLAND

The memory of Henry Sidgwick is not yet in need of revival. It lives a natural life among us, and will live so long as those who saw and heard him draw breath. Still the generations, as generations must be reckoned in this place, succeed each other rapidly, and already I may be informing, rather than reminding, some of you when I say that among his many generous acts was the endowment of a readership in English Law, of which one of his pupils was fortunate enough to be the first holder. If that pupil ventures to speak here this afternoon, it will not be unnatural that he should choose his theme from the borderland where ethical speculation marches with jurisprudence.

Ethics and Jurisprudence. — That such a borderland exists all would allow, and, as usually happens in such cases, each of the neighbouring powers is wont to assert, in practice, if not in theory, its right to define the scientific frontier. We, being English, are, so I fancy, best acquainted with the claims of ethical speculation, and in some sort prejudiced in their favour. We are proud of a long line of moralists, which has not ended in Sidgwick and Martineau and Green, in Herbert Spencer and Leslie Stephen, and we conceive that the 'jurist', if indeed such an animal exists, plays, and of right ought to play, a subordinate, if not subservient, part in the delimitation of whatever moral sciences there may happen to be. I am not sure, however, that the poor lawyer with antiquarian tastes might not take his revenge by endeavouring to explain the moral philosopher as a legal phenomenon, and by classing our specifically English addiction to ethics as a by-product of the specifically English history of English law. That statement, if it be more than the mere turning of the downtrodden worm, is obviously too large, as it is too insolent, a text for an hour's lecture. What I shall attempt will be to indicate one problem of a speculative sort, which (so it seems to me) does not get the attention that it deserves from speculative Englishmen, and does not get that attention because it is shrouded from their view by certain peculiarities of the legal system in which they live.

The Natural Person and the Corporation. — Texts, however, I will have. My first is taken from Mr Balfour. Lately in the House of Commons the Prime Minister spoke of trade unions as corporations. Perhaps, for he is an accomplished debater, he anticipated an interruption. At any rate, a distinguished lawyer on the Opposition benches interrupted him with 'The trade unions are not corporations.' 'I knew that,' retorted Mr Balfour, 'I am talking English, not law.' A long story was packed into that admirable reply.[2]

And my second text is taken from Mr Dicey, who delivered the Sidgwick lecture last year. 'When,' he said, 'a body of twenty, or two thousand, or two hundred thousand men bind themselves together to act in a particular way for some common purpose, they create a body, which by no fiction of law, but by the very nature of things, differs from the individuals of whom it is constituted'.[3] I have been waiting a long while for an English lawyer of Professor Dicey's eminence to say what he said — to talk so much 'English'. Let me repeat a few of his words with the stress where I should like it to lie: 'they create a body, which *by no fiction of law, but by the very nature of things*, differs from the individuals of whom it is constituted'. So says Blackstone's successor. Blackstone himself would, I think, have inverted that phrase, and would have ascribed to a fiction of law that phenomenon — or whatever we are to call it — which Mr Dicey ascribes to the very nature of things.

Now for a long time past the existence of this phenomenon has been recognised by lawyers, and the orthodox manner of describing it has been somewhat of this kind. Besides men or 'natural persons', law knows persons of another kind. In particular it knows the corporation, and for a multitude of purposes it treats the corporation very much as it treats the man. Like the man, the corporation is (forgive this compound adjective) a right-and-duty-bearing unit. Not all the legal propositions that are true of a man will be true of

a corporation. For example, it can neither marry nor be given
in marriage; but in a vast number of cases you can make a
legal statement about *x* and *y* which will hold good whether
these symbols stand for two men or for two corporations, or
for a corporation and a man. The University can buy land
from Downing, or hire the guildhall from the Town, or
borrow money from the London Assurance; and we may say
that *exceptis excipiendis* a court of law can treat these
transactions, these acts in the law, as if they took place
between two men, between Styles and Nokes. But further,
we have to allow that the corporation is in some sense
composed of men, and yet between the corporation and one
of its members there may exist many, perhaps most, of those
legal relationships which can exist between two human
beings. I can contract with the University: the University can
contract with me. You can contract with the Great Northern
Company as you can with the Great Eastern, though you
happen to be a shareholder in the one and not in the other.
In either case there stands opposite to you another right-and-
duty-bearing unit — might I not say another individual? — a
single 'not-yourself' that can pay damages or exact them.
You expect results of this character, and, if you did not get
them, you would think ill of law and lawyers. Indeed, I
should say that, the less we know of law, the more con-
fidently we Englishmen expect that the organised group,
whether called a corporation or not, will be treated as person:
that is, as right-and-duty-bearing unit.

Legal Orthodoxy and the Fictitious Person. — Perhaps I
can make the point clearer by referring to an old case. We are
told that in Edward IV's day the mayor and commonalty —
or, as we might be tempted to say, the municipal corporation
— of Newcastle gave a bond to the man who happened to be
mayor, he being named by his personal name, and that the
bond was held to be void because a man cannot be bound to
himself.[4] The argument that is implicit in those few words
seems to us quaint, if not sophistical. But the case does not
stand alone; far from it. If our business is with medieval
history and our aim is to re-think it before we re-present it,
here lies one of our most serious difficulties. Can we allow
the group — guild, town, village, nation — to stand over

against each and all of its members as a distinct person? To be concrete, look at Midsummer Common. It belongs, and, so far as we know, has always in some sense belonged, to the burgesses of Cambridge. But in what sense? Were they co-proprietors? were they corporators? Neither — both?

I would not trouble you with medievalism. Only this by the way: If once you become interested in the sort of history that tries to unravel these and similar problems, you will think some other sorts of history rather superficial. Perhaps you will go the length of saying that much the most interesting person that you ever knew was *persona ficta*. But my hour flies.

To steer a clear or any course is hard, for controversial rocks abound. Still, with some security we may say that at the end of the Middle Age a great change in men's thoughts about groups of men was taking place, and that the main agent in the transmutation was Roman Law. Now just how the classical jurists of Rome conceived their *corpora* and *universitates* became in the nineteenth century a much debated question. The profane outsider says of the Digest what some one said of another book:

> Hic liber est in quo quaerit sua dogmata quisque
> Invenit et pariter dogmata quisque sua.

Where people have tried to make antique texts do modern work, the natural result is what Mr Buckland has happily called 'Wardour Street Roman Law'.[5] Still, of this I suppose there can be no doubt, that there could, without undue pressure, be obtained from the Corpus Juris a doctrine of corporations, which, so far as some main outlines are concerned, is the doctrine which has ruled the modern world. Nor would it be disputed that this work was done by the legists and canonists of the Middle Age, the canonists leading the way. The group can be a person: co-ordinated, equiparated, with the man, with the natural person.

With the 'natural' person — for the personality of the *universitas*, of the corporation, is not natural — it is fictitious. This is a very important part of the canonical doctrine, first clearly proclaimed, so we are told, by the greatest lawyer that ever sat upon the chair of St Peter, Pope Innocent IV. You will recall Mr Dicey's words: 'not by fiction of law, but by the very nature of things'. Invert those words, and you will have a dogma that works like leaven in the transformation of medieval society.

If the personality of the corporation is a legal fiction, it is the gift of the prince. It is not for you and me to feign and to force our fictions upon our neighbours. 'Solus princeps fingit quod in rei veritate non est.'[6] An argument drawn from the very nature of fictions thus came to the aid of less questionably Roman doctrines about the illicitness of all associations, the existence of which the prince has not authorised. I would not exaggerate the importance of a dogma, theological or legal. A dogma is of no importance unless and until there is some great desire within it. But what was understood to be the Roman doctrine of corporations was an apt lever for those forces which were transforming the medieval nation into the modern State. The federalistic structure of medieval society is threatened. No longer can we see the body politic as *communitas communitatum*, a system of groups, each of which in its turn is a system of groups. All that stands between the State and the individual has but a derivative and precarious existence.

Do not let us at once think of England. English history can never be an elementary subject: we are not logical enough to be elementary. If we must think of England, then let us remember that we are in the presence of a doctrine which in Charles II's day condemns all — yes, all — of the citizens of London to prison for 'presuming to act as a corporation'. We may remember also how corporations appear to our absolutist Hobbes as troublesome entozoa. But it is always best to begin with France, and there, I take it, we may see the pulverising, macadamising tendency in all its glory, working from century to century, reducing to impotence, and then to nullity, all that intervenes between Man and State.

The State and the Corporation. — In this, as in some other instances, the work of the monarchy issues in the work of the revolutionary assemblies. It issues in the famous declaration of August 18, 1792: 'A State that is truly free ought not to suffer within its bosom any corporation, not even such as, being dedicated to public instruction, have merited well of the country.'[7] That was one of the mottoes of modern absolutism: the absolute State faced the absolute individual. An appreciable part of the interest of the French Revolution seems to me to be open only to those who will be at pains to give a little thought to the theory of corporations. Take, for example, those memorable debates touching ecclesiastical property. To whom belong these broad lands when you have pushed fictions aside, when you have become a truly philosophical jurist with a craving for the natural? To the nation, which has stepped into the shoes of the prince. That is at least a plausible answer, though an uncomfortable suspicion that the State itself is but a questionably real person may not be easily dispelled. And as with the churches, the universities, the trade-guilds, and the like, so also with the communes, the towns and villages. Village property — there was a great deal of village property in France — was exposed to the dilemma: it belongs to the State, or else it belongs to the now existing villagers. I doubt we Englishmen, who never clean our slates, generally know how clean the French slate was to be.

Associations in France. — Was to be, I say. Looking back now, French lawyers can regard the nineteenth century as the century of association, and, if there is to be association, if there is to be group-formation, the problem of personality cannot be evaded, at any rate if we are a logical people. Not to mislead, I must in one sentence say, that even the revolutionary legislators spared what we call partnership, and that for a long time past French law has afforded comfortable quarters for various kinds of groups, provided (but notice this) that the group's one and only object was the making of pecuniary gain. Recent writers have noticed it as a paradox that the State saw no harm in the selfish people who wanted dividends, while it had an intense dread of the comparatively unselfish people who would combine with some religious, charitable, literary, scientific, artistic purpose in view. I cannot within my few minutes be precise, but at the beginning of this twentieth century it was still a misdemeanour to belong to any unauthorised *association* having more than twenty members. A licence from the prefect, which might be obtained with some ease, made the *association* non-criminal, made it licit; but personality — 'civil personality', as they say in France — was only to be acquired with difficulty as the gift of the central government.

Now I suppose it to be notorious that during the last years of the nineteenth century law so unfavourable to liberty of association was still being maintained, chiefly, if not solely, because prominent, typically prominent, among the *associations* known to Frenchmen stood the *congrégations* — religious houses, religious orders. The question how these were to be treated divided the nation, and at last, in 1901, when a new and very important law was made about 'the contract of association', a firm line was drawn between the non-religious sheep and the religious goats. With the step then taken and the subsequent woes of the congregations I have here no concern; but the manner in which religious and other groups had previously been treated by French jurisprudence seems to me exceedingly instructive. It seems to me to prove so clearly that in a country where people take their legal theories seriously, a country where a Prime Minister will often talk law without ceasing to talk agreeable French, the question whether the group is to be, as we say, 'a person in the eye of the Law' is the question whether the group as group can enjoy more than an uncomfortable and precarious existence. I am not thinking of attacks directed against it by the State. I am thinking of collisions between it and private persons. It lives at the mercy of its neighbours, for a law-suit will dissolve it into its constituent atoms. Nor is that all. Sometimes its neighbours will have cause to complain of its legal impersonality. They will have been thinking of it as a responsible right-and-duty-bearing unit, while at the touch of law it becomes a mere many, and a practically, if not theoretically, irresponsible many.

Group-Personality. — During the nineteenth century (so I understand the case) a vast mass of experience, French, German, Belgian, Italian, and Spanish (and I might add, though the atmosphere is hazier, English and American), has been making for a result which might be stated in more than one way. (1) If the law allows men to form permanently organised groups, those groups will be for common opinion right-and-duty-bearing units; and if the law-giver will not openly treat them as such, he will misrepresent, or, as the

French say, he will 'denature' the facts: in other words, he will make a mess and call it law. (2) Group-personality is no purely legal phenomenon. The law-giver may say that it does not exist, where, as a matter of moral sentiment, it does exist. When that happens, he incurs the penalty ordained for those who ignorantly or wilfully say the thing that is not. If he wishes to smash a group, let him smash it, send the policeman, raid the rooms, impound the minute-book, fine, and imprison; but if he is going to tolerate the group, he must recognise its personality, for otherwise he will be dealing wild blows which may fall on those who stand outside the group as well as those who stand within it. (3) For the morality of common sense the group is person, is right-and-duty-bearing unit. Let the moral philosopher explain this, let him explain it as illusion, let him explain it away; but he ought not to leave it unexplained, nor, I think, will he be able to say that it is an illusion which is losing power, for, on the contrary, it seems to me to be persistently and progressively triumphing over certain philosophical and theological prejudices.

You know that classical distribution of Private Law under three grand rubrics — Persons, Things, Actions. Half a century ago the first of these three titles seemed to be almost vanishing from civilised jurisprudence. No longer was there much, if anything, to be said of exceptional classes, of nobles, clerics, monks, serfs, slaves, excommunicates or outlaws. Children there might always be, ˎand lunatics; but women had been freed from tutelage. The march of the progressive societies was, as we all know, from status to contract. And now? And now that forlorn old title is wont to introduce us to ever new species and new genera of persons, to vivacious controversy, to teeming life; and there are many to tell us that the line of advance is no longer from status to contract, but through contract to something that contract cannot explain, and for which our best, if an inadequate, name is the personality of the organised group.

Fact of Fiction? — Theorising, of course, there has been. I need not say so, nor that until lately it was almost exclusively German. Our neighbours' conception of the province of jurisprudence has its advantages as well as its disadvantages. On the one hand, ethical speculation (as we might call it) of a

very interesting kind was until these last days too often
presented in the unattractive guise of Wardour Street Roman
Law, or else, raising the Germanistic cry of 'Loose from
Rome!' it plunged into an exposition of medieval charters.
On the other hand, the theorising is often done by men who
have that close grasp of concrete modern fact which comes of
a minute and practical study of legal systems. Happily it is no
longer necessary to go straight to Germany. That struggle
over 'the contract of association' to which I have alluded,
those woes of the 'congregations' of which all have heard,
invoked foreign learning across the border, and now we may
read in lucid French of the various German theories. Good
reading I think it; and what interests me especially is that the
French lawyer, with all his orthodoxy (legal orthodoxy) and
conservatism, with all his love of clarity and abhorrence of
mysticism, is often compelled to admit that the traditional
dogmas of the law-school have broken down. Much disin-
clined though he may be to allow the group a real will of its
own, just as really real as the will of a man, still he has to
admit that if *n* men unite themselves in an organised body,
jurisprudence, unless it wishes to pulverise the group, must
see *n* + 1 persons. And that for the mere lawyer should I
think be enough. 'Of heaven and hell he has no power to
sing.' and he might content himself with a phenomenal reality — such reality, for example, as the lamp-post has for the
idealistic ontologist. Still, we do not like to be told that we
are dealing in fiction, even if it be added that we needs must
feign, and the thought will occur to us that a fiction that we
needs must feign is somehow or another very like the simple
truth.

Why we English people are not interested in a problem
that is being seriously discussed in many other lands, that is a
question to which I have tried to provide some sort of answer
elsewhere.[8] It is a long, and you would think it a very dreary,
story about the most specifically English of all our legal
institutes; I mean the trust. All that I can say here is that the
device of building a wall of trustees enabled us to construct
bodies which were not technically corporations and which
yet would be sufficiently protected from the assaults of
individualistic theory. The personality of such bodies — so I

should put it — though explicitly denied by lawyers, was on the whole pretty well recognised in practice. That something of this sort happened you might learn from one simple fact. For some time past we have had upon our statute book the term 'unincorporate body'. Suppose that a Frenchman saw it, what would he say? 'Unincorporate body: inanimate soul! No wonder your Prime Minister, who is a philosopher, finds it hard to talk English and talk law at the same time.'

One result of this was, so I fancy, that the speculative Englishman could not readily believe that in this quarter there was anything to be explored except some legal trickery unworthy of exploration. The lawyer assured him that it was so, and he saw around him great and ancient, flourishing and wealthy groups — the Inns of Court at their head — which, so the lawyer said, were not persons. To have cross-examined the lawyer over the bodiliness of his 'unincorporate body' might have brought out some curious results; but such a course was hardly open to those who shared our wholesome English contempt for legal technique.

The Ultimate Moral Unit. — Well, I must finish; and yet perhaps I have not succeeded in raising just the question that I wanted to ask. Can I do that in two or three last sentences? It is a moral question, and therefore I will choose my hypothetical case from a region in which our moral sentiments are not likely to be perplexed by legal technique. My organised group shall be a sovereign state. Let us call it Nusquamia. Like many other sovereign states, it owes money, and I will suppose that you are one of its creditors. You are not receiving the expected interest and there is talk of repudiation. That being so, I believe that you will be, and indeed I think that you ought to be, indignant, morally, righteously indignant. Now the question that I want to raise is this: Who is it that really owes you money? Nusquamia. Granted, but can you convert the proposition that Nusquamia owes you money into a series of propositions imposing duties on certain human beings that are now in existence? The task will not be easy. Clearly you do not think that every Nusquamian owes you some aliquot share of the debt. No one thinks in that way. The debt of Venezuela is not owed by Fulano y Zutano and the rest of them. Nor, I think, shall we get much good out of the word 'collectively', which is the smudgiest word in the English language, for the largest 'collection' of zeros is only zero. I do not wish to say that I have suggested an impossible task, and that the right-and-duty-bearing group must be for the philosopher an ultimate and unanalysable moral unit: as ultimate and unanalysable, I mean, as is the man. Only if that task can be performed, I think that in the interests of jurisprudence and of moral philosophy it is eminently worthy of circumspect performance. As to our national law, it has sound instincts, and muddles along with semi-personality and demi-semi-personality towards convenient conclusions. Still, I cannot think that Parliament's timid treatment of the trade unions has been other than a warning, or that it was a brilliant day in our legal annals when the affairs of the Free Church of Scotland were brought before the House of Lords, and the dead hand fell with a resounding slap upon the living body. As to philosophy, that is no affair of mine. I speak with conscious ignorance and unfeigned humility; only of this I feel moderately sure, that those who are to tell us of the very nature of things and the very nature of persons will not be discharging their duties to the full unless they come to close terms with that triumphant fiction, if fiction it be, of which I have said in your view more than too much, and in my own view less than too little.

NOTES

1. The Sidgwick Lecture, 1903, delivered at Newnham College, Cambridge, and printed in H. A. L. Fisher (ed.), *The Collected Papers of Frederic William Maitland* (Cambridge University Press, 1911) vol. iii pp. 304-19.
2. The *Standard*, 23 April 1904. *Mr Balfour:* 'The mere fact that funds can be used, or are principally used, for benefit purposes, is surely not of itself a sufficient reason for saying that trade unions, and trade unions alone, out of all the corporations in the country, commercial——' *Sir R. Reid:* 'The trade unions are not corporations.' *Mr Balfour:* 'I know; I am talking English, not law' (*cheers and laughter*).
3. Professor Dicey's lecture on the Combination Laws is printed in *Harvard Law Review*, xvii 511.
4. Year Book, 21 Edw. IV, f. 68: 'Come fuit ajudgé en le cas del Maior de Newcastle ou le Maior et le Cominalty fist un obligation a mesme le person que fuit Maior par son propre nosme, et pur

ceo que il mesme fuit Maior, et ne puit faire obligation a luy mesme, il [=l'obligation] fuit tenus voide.'

5. Buckland, 'Wardour Street Roman Law', *Law Quarterly Review*, xvii 179.
6. Lucas de Penna, cited in Gierke, *Das deutsche Genossenschafts-recht*, iii 371.
7. 'Considérant qu'un État vraiment libre ne doit souffrir dans son sein aucune corporation, pas même celles qui, vouées à l'enseigne-ment public, ont bien mérité de la patrie.'
8. Maitland, 'Trust und Korporation', Wien, 1904 (from *Grünhut's Zeitschrift fur das Privat- und Öffentliche-Recht*, vol. xxxii). See below, p. 321.

Bibliography

J. E. E. D. Acton, *Essays on Freedom and Power*, ed. G. Himmelfarb (Boston: Beacon, 1956).

———*The History of Freedom* (London: Macmillan, 1907).

The Letters of Lord Acton to Mary Gladstone (London: Allen and Unwin, 1904).

Aristotle, *Politics*, ed. E. Barker (London: Oxford University Press, 1948).

J. Austin, *The Province of Jurisprudence Determined* (London: Murray, 1861).

W. Bagehot, *Works* (London: Longmans, 1915).

E. Barker, *Age and Youth* (London: Oxford University Press, 1953).

——— *Political Thought in England 1848-1914* (London: Butterworth, 1928).

G. K. A. Bell (ed.), *The Meaning of the Creed* (London: SPCK, 1921).

H. Belloc, *The Servile State* (London: Constable, 1927).

——— and C. Chesterton, *The Party System* (London: Swift, 1911).

C. Benoist, *La politique* (Paris: Chailley, 1894).

A. F. Bentley, *The Process of Government* (Chicago, University of Chicago Press, 1908).

I. Berlin, *Four Essays on Liberty* (London: Oxford University Press, 1969).

Eduard Bernstein, *Evolutionary Socialism* (New York: Schocken, 1961).

J. F. Bethune-Baker, *The Miracle of Christianity* (London: Longmans, 1914).

F. H. Bradley, *Ethical Studies* (London: King, 1876).

J. Bryce, *Studies in History and Jurisprudence* (Oxford: Clarendon, 1901).

H. Butterfield, *The Historical Development of the Principle of Toleration in British Life* (London: Epworth, 1957).

N. Carpenter, *Guild Socialism* (New York: Appleton, 1922).

Church Information Office, *Church and State* (London: 1970).

K. Coates and T. Topham (eds.), *Workers' Control* (London: Panther, 1970).

M. Cohen, *Reason and Nature* (London: Kegan Paul, 1931).

G. D. H. Cole, *Chaos and Order in Industry* (London: Methuen, 1920).

——— *Guild Socialism Restated* (London: Parsons, 1920).

——— *Labour in the Commonwealth* (London: Swathmore, 1918).

——— *Self-Government in Industry* (London: Bell, 1917).

——— *Social Theory* (London: Methuen, 1920).

Margaret Cole, *The Story of Fabian Socialism* (New York: John Wiley, 1964).

W. E. Connolly (ed.), *The Bias of Pluralism* (New York: Atherton, 1969).

L. Creighton, *The Life and Letters of Mandell Creighton* (London: Longmans, 1904).

B. Crick, *In Defence of Politics* (Harmondsworth: Penguin, 1964).

R. Dahrendorf, *Class and Class Conflict in Industrial Society* (London: Routledge, 1959).

Joseph de Maistre, *Du pape* (Paris: Charpentier, 1845).

P. Derrick, *Lost Property* (London: Dobson, 1947).

P. Devlin, *The Enforcement of Morals* (London: Oxford University Press, 1965).

J. Dewey, *Reconstruction in Philosophy* (London: University of London Press, 1921).

A. V. Dicey, *An Introduction to the Study of the Law of the Constitution* (London: 1908).

L. Duguit, *Law in the Modern State* (London: Allen and Unwin, 1921).

L. Duguit, *L'état, le droit objectif et la loi positive* (Paris: Fontemoing, 1901).

E. Durkheim, *The Division of Labor* (New York: Macmillan, 1933).

F. Dvornik, *National Churches and the Church Universal* (London: Dacre Press, 1944).

T. S. Eliot, *Notes towards the Definition of Culture* (London: Faber, 1967).

W. Y. Elliott, *The Pragmatic Revolt in Politics* (New York: Macmillan, 1928).

A. Farrer, *The Freedom of the Will* (London: Black, 1958).

J. H. Fichter, *Sociology* (Chicago: University of Chicago Press, 1957).

J. N. Figgis, *Antichrist and Other Sermons* (London: Longmans, 1913).

—————— *Christianity and History* (London: Finch, 1905).

—————— *Churches in the Modern State* (London: Longmans, 1913).

—————— *The Divine Right of Kings* (Cambridge: Cambridge University Press, 1914).

—————— *The Fellowship of the Mystery* (London: Longmans, 1915).

—————— *The Gospel and Human Needs* (London: Longmans, 1909).

—————— *Hopes for English Religion* (London: Longmans, 1919).

—————— *Political Aspects of St. Augustine's 'City of God'* (London: Longmans, 1921)

—————— *Studies of Political Thought from Gerson to Grotius 1414-1625* (Cambridge: Cambridge University Press, 1916).

—————— *The Will to Freedom* (London: Longmans, 1917).

M. P. Follett, *The New State* (New York: Longmans, 1918).

P. T. Forsyth, *The Principle of Authority* (London: Hodder and Stoughton, 1952).

—————— *Theology in Church and State* (London: Hodder and Stoughton, 1915).

J. S. Furnivall, *Colonial Policy and Practice* (Cambridge: Cambridge University Press, 1948).

Otto von Gierke, *Das deutsch Genossenschaftsrecht* (Berlin: Weidmann, 1868-1913).

—————— *The Development of Political Theory* (London: Allen and Unwin, 1939).

—————— *Die Genossenschaftstheorie und die deutsche Rechtsprechung* (Berlin: Weidmann, 1887).

────── *Natural Law and the Theory of Society* (Cambridge: Cambridge University Press, 1934).

────── *Political Theories of the Middle Age* (Cambridge: Cambridge University Press, 1900).

────── *Das Wesen der menschlichen Verbände* (Berlin: Schade, 1902).

S. T. Glass, *The Responsible Society* (London: Longmans, 1966).

Charles Gore, *The Basis of Anglican Fellowship in Faith and Organization* (London: Mowbray, 1914).

L. C. B. Gower, *The Principles of Modern Company Law* (London: Stevens, 1957).

G. Goyau, *Ketteler* (Paris: Bloud, 1907).

T. H. Green, *Lectures on the Principles of Political Obligation* (London: Longmans, 1895).

H. M. Gwatkin, *The Bishop of Oxford's Open Letter* (London: Longmans, 1914).

R. M. Hare, *The Language of Morals* (London: Oxford University Press, 1952).

H. L. A. Hart, *Law, Liberty and Morality* (London: Oxford University Press, 1963).

────── *The Concept of Law* (Oxford: Clarendon, 1963).

G. W. F. Hegel, *The Philosophy of Right* (London: Oxford University Press, 1942).

Hegel's Political Writings (Knox and Pelczynski, eds.) (Oxford: Clarendon, 1964).

R. Hinden (ed.), *Fabian Colonial Essays* (London: Allen and Unwin, 1945).

T. Hobbes, *Leviathan* (Oxford: Blackwell, 1946).

L. T. Hobhouse, *The Metaphysical Theory of the State* (London: Allen and Unwin, 1918).

J. A. Hobson and M. Ginsberg, *L. T. Hobhouse* (London: Allen and Unwin, 1931).

S. G. Hobson, *National Guilds and the State* (London: Bell, 1920).

M. de W. Howe (ed.), *Holmes-Laski Letters* (London: Oxford University Press, 1953).

────── (ed.), *Pollock-Holmes Letters* (Cambridge: Cambridge University Press, 1942).

K. C. Hsiao, *Political Pluralism* (London: Kegan Paul, 1927).

W. James, *A Pluralistic Universe* (London: Longmans, 1909).

W. K. Jordan, *The Development of Religious Toleration in England* (London: Allen and Unwin, 1932).

H. M. Kallen, *Cultural Pluralism and the American Ideal* (Philadelphia: University of Pennsylvania Press, 1956).

H. S. Kariel, *The Decline of American Pluralism* (Stanford: Stanford University Press, 1967).

Clark Kerr, *Industrial Relations and the Liberal Pluralist* (Berkeley: Institute of Industrial Relations, 1955).

W. E. von Ketteler, *Die Arbeiterfrage und das Christenthum* (Mainz: Kirchheim, 1864).

P. King, *Fear of Power* (London: Cass 1967).

L. Kuper and M. G. Smith (eds.), *Pluralism in Africa* (Berkeley and Los Angeles: University of California Press, 1969).

H. J. Laski, *Authority in the Modern State* (New Haven: Yale University Press, 1919).

————— *A Grammar of Politics* (London: Allen and Unwin, 1925).

————— *Introduction to Contemporary Politics* (Seattle: University of Washington Bookstore, 1939).

————— *Studies in the Problem of Sovereignty* (New Haven: Yale University Press, 1917).

E. Latham, *The Group Basis of Politics* (Ithaca: Cornell University Press, 1952).

J. D. Lewis, *The Genossenschaft Theory of Otto von Gierke* (Madison: University of Wisconsin Press, 1935).

W. Lippmann, *A Preface to Morals* (London: Allen and Unwin, 1929).

D. Lloyd, *The Law Relating to Unincorporated Associations* (London: Sweet and Maxwell, 1938).

H. M. Magid, *English Political Pluralism* (New York: Columbia University Press, 1941).

H. Maine, *Lectures on the Early History of Institutions* (London: Murray, 1893).

————— *Popular Government* (London: Murray, 1890).

F. W. Maitland, *Collected Papers* (Cambridge: Cambridge University Press, 1911).

J. E. F. Mann *et al.*, *The Real Democracy* (London: Longmans, 1913).

A. J. Mason *et al.*, *Our Place In Christendom* (London: Longmans, 1916).

Robert Michels, *Political Parties* (New York: Collier, 1962).

J. S. Mill, *On Liberty* (London: Watts, 1903).

————— *The Principles of Political Economy* (London: Longmans 1883).

B. Mitchell, *Law, Morality and Religion in a Secular Society* (London: Oxford University Press, 1970).

S. Mogi, *Otto von Gierke* (London: King, 1932).

————— *The Problem of Federalism* (London: Allen and Unwin, 1931).

J. H. Newman, *A Letter addressed to his Grace the Duke of Norfolk on the Occasion of Mr Gladstone's Recent Expostulation* (London: Pickering, 1875).

D. Nicholls (ed.), *Church and State in Britain since 1820* (London: Routledge, 1967).

H. R. Niebuhr, *The Kingdom of God in America* (Chicago: Willett, 1937).

P. H. Nowell-Smith, *Ethics* (Harmondsworth: Penguin, 1954).

S. L. Ollard *et al.*, *Dictionary of English Church History* (London: Mowbray, 1912).

S. Orwell and I. Angus (eds.), *The Collected Essays, Journalism and Letters of George Orwell* (Harmondsworth: Penguin 1970).

J. R. Pennock and J. W. Chapman (eds.), *Voluntary Associations* (New York: Atherton, 1969).

F. Pollock, *Essays in the Law* (London: Macmillan, 1922).

————— *A First Book of Jurisprudence* (London: Macmillan, 1923).

G. L. Prestige, *The Life of Charles Gore, A Great Englishman* (London: Heinemann, 1935).

H. Preuss, *Geminde, Staat, Reich* (Berlin, 1889).

P. J. Proudhon, *L'idée générale de la révolution du 19e siècle* (Paris, 1929).

————— *Du principe fédératif* (Paris, 1921).

K. Rahner, *Bishops: their Status and Function* (London: Burns and Oates, 1964).

——— *Theological Investigations* (London: Darton, Longman and Todd, 1962f).

H. M. Relton, *Church and State* (London: Allan, 1936).

D. G. Ritchie, *Darwin and Hegel* (London: Sonnenschein, 1893).

——— *The Principles of State Interference* (London: Sonnenschein,, 1891).

G. Ritter, *The Corrupting Influence of Power* (Hadleigh: Tower Bridge Publications, 1952).

L. Rockow, *Contemporary Political Thought in England* (London: Parsons, 1925).

J. J. Rousseau, *Social Contract and Discourses* (London: Dent, 1913).

V. Rubin (ed.), *Social and Cultural Pluralism in the Caribbean* (New York: New York Academy of Sciences, 1960).

B. Russell, *Democracy and Direct Action* (London: Independent Labour Party, 1919).

——— *Political Ideals* (New York: Century, 1917).

——— *Principles of Social Reconstruction* (London: Allen and Unwin, 1916).

Salmond on Jurisprudence (ed. G. Williams) (London: Sweet and Maxwell, 1957).

W. Sanday, *Bishop Gore's Challenge to Criticism* (London: Longmans, 1914).

F. C. von Savigny, *Jural Relations* (London: Wildy, 1884).

——— *System of Modern Roman Law* (Madras: 1867).

J. W. Scott, *Syndicalism and Philosophical Realism* (London: Black, 1919).

A. A. Seaton, *The Theory of Toleration under the Later Stuarts* (Cambridge: Cambridge University Press, 1911).

P. Selznick, *Law, Society and Industrial Justice* (New York: Russell Sage, 1969).

——— *TVA and the Grass Roots* (Berkeley: University of California Press, 1949).

G. B. Shaw (ed.), *Fabian Essays* (London: Fabian Society, 1889).

E. Shils, *The Torment of Secrecy* (Glencoe: The Free Press, 1956).

H. Sidgwick, *The Elements of Politics* (London: Macmillan, 1908).

——— *The Ethics of Conformity and Subscription* (London: Williams & Norgate 1870).

——— *The Methods of Ethics* (London: Macmillan, 1890).

——— *Practical Ethics* (London: Sonnenschein, 1898).

G. Simmel, *Conflict* and *The Web of Group Affiliations* (Glencoe: The Free Press, 1955).

H. A. Smith, *The Law of Associations* (Oxford: Clarendon, 1914).

G. Sorel, *Réflexions sur la violence* (Paris: Rivière, 1910).

W. J. Stankiewicz (ed.), *In defence of Sovereignty* (London: Oxford University Press, 1969).

L. S. Stebbing, *Ideals and Illusions* (London: Watts, 1944).

J. F. Stephen, *Liberty Equality Fraternity* (London: Smith Elder, 1874).

A. P. Stokes, *Church and State in the United States* (New York: Harper, 1950).

P. F. Strawson, *Individuals* (London: Methuen, 1959).

A. de Tocqueville, *Journeys to England and Ireland* (London: Faber, 1958).

Ernst Troeltsch, *The Social Teaching of the Christian Churches* (London: Allen and Unwin, 1931).

J. Tussman, *Obligation and the Body Politic* (New York: Oxford University Press, 1960).

George Tyrrell, *The Church and the Future* (London: Priory Press, 1910).

A. B. Ulam, *The Philosophical Foundations of English Socialism* (Cambridge, Mass.: Harvard University Press, 1951).

J. O. Urmson, *Philosophical Analysis* (Oxford: Clarendon, 1956).

L. C. Webb (ed.), *Legal Personality and Political Pluralism* (Carlton: Melbourne University Press, 1958).

S. Webb, *Towards Social Democracy* (London: Fabian Society, 1919).

M. Wiles, *The Remaking of Christian Doctrine* (London: SCM Press, 1974).

J. Wisdom, *Philosophy and Psycho-analysis* (Oxford: Blackwell, 1953).

R. P. Wolff, *The Poverty of Liberalism* (Boston: Beacon, 1968).

B. Zylstra, *From Pluralism to Collectivism* (Assen: van Gorcum, 1968).

Index